Shining Star B

Workbook

Anna Uhl Chamot

Pam Hartmann

Jann Huizenga

with

Steve Sloan

Longman

longman.com

Shining Star ★ B

Workbook

Pearson Education, 10 Bank Street, White Plains, NY 10606

Workbook consultant: Steve Sloan

Vice president, director of instructional design: Allen Ascher
Editorial director: Ed Lamprich
Acquisitions editor: Amanda Rappaport Dobbins
Project manager: Susan Saslow
Workbook manager: Donna Schaffer
Senior development editor: Susan Clarke Ball
Vice president, director of design and production: Rhea Banker
Executive managing editor: Linda Moser
Production manager: Ray Keating
Senior production editor: Sylvia Dare
Director of manufacturing: Patrice Fraccio
Senior manufacturing buyer: Edith Pullman
Photo research: Kirchoff/Wohlberg, Inc.
Design and production: Kirchoff/Wohlberg, Inc.
Cover design: Rhea Banker, Tara Mayer
Text font: 11/14 Franklin Gothic
Acknowledgments: See page 169
Illustrations: 21, 22 Mapping Specialists; 38 Leslie Evans; 47, 75 left Inklink
    Firenze; 95 Tom Leonard; 101, 108 Jean & Mon-sien Tseng; 104, 105, 106
    Mike DiGiorgio; 110, 111 John Hovell; 156 Ron Tanovitz.
Photos: 10, 11, 14, 18, 24, 28, 30, 31, 46, 52, 59 Dorling Kindersley; 60
    Bettmann/CORBIS; 67 George H.H. Huey/CORBIS; 70 Amy Arbus; 73
    Stone/Getty Images; 74, 83 Dorling Kindersley; 75 middle & right Dorling
    Kindersley; 88 John Mead/SPL/Photo Researchers; 98, 112, 116, 123,
    128, 136, 139, 144 Dorling Kindersley; 150 The De Morgan Foundation,
    London/The Bridgeman Art Library; 154, 158 Dorling Kindersley; 164 Tony
    Freeman/PhotoEdit.

ISBN: 0-13-049959-5

Printed in the United States of America
    4 5 6 7 8 9 10–BAH–08 07 06 05 04

Welcome to *Shining Star's* Workbook. Exercises in each unit of this book will help you practice the skills and strategies you've already learned throughout the *Shining Star* program. You'll have fun completing crossword puzzles as you build your vocabulary. Other activities will help you apply reading strategies and practice language-development skills in grammar, spelling, writing, proofreading, and editing.

To help you get the most out of your *Shining Star* reading experiences, we've added an exciting feature—Reader's Companion. The Reader's Companion activities will help you better understand and explore the "Connect to Literature" and "Connect to Content" selections in your Student Book.

Reader's Companion begins with a summary that tells you what the selection is about before you read. Then a visual summary helps you focus on the main ideas and details, as well as the organization of each selection. Use What You Know lets you explore your own knowledge or experience before you read. You'll apply reading strategies that you've already learned, show that you know about the kind of selection you're reading—whether it's an informational text or a song. You'll check your comprehension or understanding of a selection and enjoy using literary elements. You'll find write-on-lines for recording your answers. Whenever you see the Mark the Text symbol, you'll know that you should underline, circle, or mark the text. We hope you enjoy choosing from the many creative activities designed to suit your own learning styles.

After reading, Reader's Companion will give you opportunities to retell selections in creative ways—using your own words. You can also write your thoughts and reactions to the selection. Then you can comment on how certain skills and strategies were helpful to you. Thinking about a skill will help you apply it to other reading situations.

We hope you'll enjoy showing what you know as you complete the many and varied activities included in your *Shining Star* Workbook.

CONTENTS

CONTENTS

CONTENTS

Copyright © 2004 by Pearson Education, Inc.

UNIT 1 Journeys of Discovery

PART 1

Contents

VOCABULARY

Use with textbook page 5.

Read each sentence. Then circle the letter next to the word that is closest in meaning to the underlined word.

1. The <u>climate</u> in Texas is much warmer than the climate in Maine.

    a. plants   b. rocks   c. weather   d. forests

2. Our <u>environment</u> is made up of all the things that surround us.

    a. tradition   b. relationships   c. harvest   d. surroundings

3. Plants that don't need water grow well in <u>arid</u> places.

    a. humid   b. wet   c. dry   d. rainy

4. The <u>region</u> of the United States that I like the most is the Southwest.

    a. state   b. area   c. capital   d. beaches

5. <u>Nomads</u> are people who have no permanent home and move from place to place.

    a. wanderers   b. mammals   c. herbivores   d. folk

Read the clues. Use the words in the box to complete the crossword puzzle. (Hint: You will not use all the words, and you will not use any word twice.)

| region | nomads | campsite | tribe | irrigate | native | climate | environment |

ACROSS

1. provide plants with water from another place

4. the typical weather of a certain area

5. section or area

DOWN

2. conditions around an animal or plant

3. group of people who are related, speak the same language, and have the same customs

VOCABULARY BUILDING

Understanding Number Words and Ordinals

Use **number words** when you want to tell *exactly how many of something*. For example, *four groups*. Use **ordinals** when you want to tell *where something is in a series*. For example, *the fourth group*. Look at the chart below.

Number Words		Ordinals	
1	one	1st	first
2	two	2nd	second
3	three	3rd	third
4	four	4th	fourth
5	five	5th	fifth
10	ten	10th	tenth
25	twenty-five	25th	twenty-fifth
50	fifty	50th	fiftieth
100	one hundred	100th	one hundredth
1,000	one thousand	1,000th	one thousandth

Read each sentence. Then decide whether a *number word* or an *ordinal* should be used in the sentence. Circle the correct answer.

Example: The (three/(third)) region we studied was the Southwest.

1. (Thirty/Thirtieth) tribes lived in the Plains.

2. The (one/first) settlers were known as the Temple Mound Builders.

3. I like the (two/second) song.

4. European settlers called them the "(Five/Fifth) Civilized Tribes."

5. The history of the Pueblo goes back (two thousand/two thousandth) years.

Write a sentence using the underlined word.

Example: <u>fifth</u> *My sister is the fifth person in my family to go to college.*

6. <u>twelve</u> _____

7. <u>fourth</u> _____

8. <u>nine</u> _____

9. <u>hundredth</u> _____

10. <u>one thousand</u> _____

READING STRATEGY

Use with textbook page 5.

Previewing and Predicting

Previewing a text helps you understand it better. Good readers always look over a text before they begin reading. This gives them an idea of what the text will be about.

When you preview a text, think about what you already know about the subject. Look at the title and headings. Also look at any pictures, photographs, graphs, charts, or maps. Use this information to **predict** what the text is probably about.

1. Look at "The First Americans" on pages 6–11 in your textbook. What do you learn from reading the title of the article? _____

_____

_____

_____

2. Read the headings of the article. What do the headings have in common?

_____

_____

_____

3. Now look at the pictures on pages 8–9 in your textbook. Write two sentences about the pictures. _____

_____

_____

_____

4. What do you think this article is about? _____

_____

_____

5. What do you already know about this subject? _____

_____

_____

_____

Use with textbook pages 14–16.

Summary: "This Land Is Your Land" and "Roll On, Columbia"

Woody Guthrie wrote these two folk songs to express his feelings about the United States. "This Land Is Your Land" describes his travels from coast to coast, through forests, deserts, and fields, and says that the nation belongs to everyone. "Roll On, Columbia" tells how the mighty Columbia River benefits the Pacific Northwest.

Visual Summary

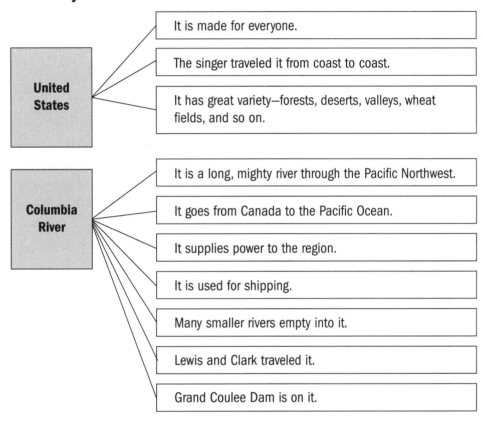

United States
- It is made for everyone.
- The singer traveled it from coast to coast.
- It has great variety—forests, deserts, valleys, wheat fields, and so on.

Columbia River
- It is a long, mighty river through the Pacific Northwest.
- It goes from Canada to the Pacific Ocean.
- It supplies power to the region.
- It is used for shipping.
- Many smaller rivers empty into it.
- Lewis and Clark traveled it.
- Grand Coulee Dam is on it.

Use What You Know

List three places or kinds of landscapes that you think of when you think of the United States.

1. _____

2. _____

3. _____

Text Structure: Song

Like many poems, most songs are arranged in groups of lines called "stanzas." A chorus is a special stanza repeated throughout the song. The other stanzas are often called verses. Underline the chorus in "This Land Is Your Land." How many verses are there?

MARK THE TEXT

_____

_____

_____

Reading Strategy: Making Inferences

An inference is a conclusion you draw from details in a selection and your own outside knowledge. Circle four places mentioned in the second and third line of the chorus. Using the details of the song and your own knowledge of geography, explain why the singer chooses these locations.

MARK THE TEXT

_____

_____

_____

This Land Is Your Land

Chorus:

This land is your land, this land is my land
From California to the New York Island,
From the redwood forest to the gulfstream waters,
This land was made for you and me.

Verses:

As I went walking that ribbon of highway
I saw above me that endless skyway,
I saw below me that golden valley,
This land was made for you and me.

I've roamed and rambled, and I followed my
    footsteps
To the sparkling sands of her diamond deserts,
All around me a voice was sounding,
This land was made for you and me.

When the sun came shining, then I was strolling,
And the wheat fields waving, and the dust clouds
    rolling,
A voice was chanting as the fog was lifting,
This land was made for you and me.

Woody Guthrie

---

land, country
ribbon of highway, long, narrow road, like a ribbon
endless, continuing; without end
roamed and rambled, moved freely through a wide area without any special purpose or goal
strolling, walking without a purpose (like *rambling*)
chanting, repeating a word or phrase again and again

Roll On, Columbia

Chorus:

Roll on, Columbia, roll on,

Roll on, Columbia, roll on,

Your power is turning our darkness to dawn,

So roll on, Columbia, roll on.

Verses:

Green Douglas firs where the waters break through,

Down the wild mountains and valleys she flew,

Canadian Northwest to the ocean so blue,

So roll on, Columbia, roll on.

_____

roll on, continue to move
power, energy
dawn, sunrise; daybreak

Choose one and complete:

1. Draw a picture of one of the scenes mentioned in "This Land Is Your Land."
2. Draw a map showing the travels of the singer. Label the places he visits, and show his possible route. Include labels for some of the less specific places in the song—for example, choose any desert area to label "diamond deserts" and any wheat-growing region to label "wheat fields waving." Use an atlas or the Internet to help you research where to put your labels.
3. From your library or an Internet music site or the audio program for this series, find and listen to a recording of "This Land Is Your Land." Describe the mood or feeling that the song creates for you when the words are put to music.

Comprehension Check

In the last stanza of "This Land Is Your Land," underline the line that has been repeated throughout the song. Explain in your own words the point that the singer is making with that line.

MARK THE TEXT

_____

_____

Literary Element: Alliteration

Alliteration is the use of the same sounds at the beginnings of nearby words—like the *d* sounds in "diamond deserts." Circle an example of alliteration in the last stanza of "This Land Is Your Land" and another in the chorus of "Roll On, Columbia." Why do you think songs often use alliteration?

MARK THE TEXT

_____

_____

_____

Reading Strategy: Making Inferences

In "Roll On, Columbia," underline the line in the chorus that tells what the Columbia River's power is doing. What use of the river do you think the songwriter really is talking about?

MARK THE TEXT

_____

_____

Comprehension Check

Underline the rivers that the song says add power to the Columbia River. Explain how these rivers might add power to the Columbia.

MARK THE TEXT

_____

_____

Text Structure: Song

Many songs use rhyme at the ends of lines, or repeat words or sounds in words. Words rhyme when they end in the same sounds. Sometimes, in poems, sounds are repeated, as with *white* and *tried*, which have the same middle sound. Sometimes, the same word is repeated at the end of lines. Circle the words that rhyme, that are repeated, or that have the same middle sounds at the ends of lines in this song. Why do you think songs often use rhyming words, repeated words, or words with the same sounds?

MARK THE TEXT

_____

_____

Reading Strategy: Making Inferences

Underline the words that tell about why the Grand Coulee Dam was built. What uses of the dam do you think these words are talking about?

MARK THE TEXT

_____

Many great rivers add power to you
The Yakima, Snake, and the Klickitat too,
Sandy Willamette and Hood River too,
So roll on, Columbia, roll on.

Tom Jefferson's vision would not let him rest,
An empire he saw in the Pacific Northwest,
Sent Lewis and Clark and they did the rest,
So roll on, Columbia, roll on.

At Bonneville now there are ships in the locks
The waters have risen and cleared all the rocks,
Shiploads of plenty will steam past the docks,
So roll on, Columbia, roll on.

And on up the river is Grand Coulee Dam,
The mightiest thing ever built by a man,
To run the great factories and water the land,
So roll on, Columbia, roll on.

Woody Guthrie

Ludlow Music, Inc. "Roll On, Columbia," words by Woody Guthrie. Music based on "Goodnight, Irene" by Huddie Ledbetter and John A. Lomax. TRO-© Copyright 1936 (Renewed) 1957 (Renewed) 1963 Ludlow Music, Inc., New York, NY. Used by permission.

_____

vision, idea or plan for the future
empire, group of countries or peoples ruled by one government
locks, parts of a river enclosed by gates on either end so that the water level can be increased or decreased to raise or lower boats
docks, places where ships stop and people can get on or off
mightiest, strongest

Retell It!

Retell the information in one of these songs in the form of a travel ad. Try to persuade people to visit the Columbia River or the places in "This Land Is Your Land."

_____

_____

_____

_____

_____

_____

_____

Reader's Response

Which of these two songs did you like better? Why?

_____

_____

_____

_____

Think About the Skill

How did making inferences help you better understand the songs?

_____

_____

_____

_____

_____

_____

GRAMMAR

Use with textbook page 18.

Using Pronouns

Pronouns are used to replace nouns. They can be subjects or objects, and they can be singular or plural. The pronoun must always agree with the noun that it replaces.

The **Northeast** had great forests.
singular

It also had many rivers and lakes.
singular

Many **tribes** lived in the Northeast.
plural

They hunted deer and fished in the lakes.
plural

	Subject Pronouns	Object Pronouns
Singular	I, you, he, she, it	me, you, him, her, it
Plural	We, you, they	us, you, them

A **subject pronoun** replaces or refers to a noun that is the subject of a sentence. **The Plains** stretch north to south for 2,000 miles. **They** are flat, grassy lands.

An **object pronoun** replaces or refers to a noun that is the object (after the verb). The Pueblo performed a special **ceremony.** The Pueblo performed **it** during the dry season.

Read the sentence pairs below. Circle each pronoun in the second sentence. Underline the noun it refers to or replaces. Follow the example.

Example: Many people love to visit the <u>Southwest</u>. (It) is the home of many Native American tribes.

1. The Navajo came to the Southwest in about 1400. They lived in what is now northern Arizona and New Mexico.

2. The Spanish brought horses to the Americas. The Navajo and Apache learned to breed them.

3. Each family had a totem pole. It was carved out of wood.

4. Temple Mound Builders built flat-topped mounds. People still come to see them today.

5. The buffalo was an important animal. It provided meat for food and skins for drums, clothing, and tepees.

GRAMMAR

Use after the lesson on adjective placement.

Adjective Placement

An **adjective** is a word that describes a person, place, or thing. It answers the questions *What kind? Which one?* or *How many?* Adjectives usually come right before the nouns they describe. Adjectives do not change when they are used with plural nouns. Look at the examples below.

    blue ocean   **wild** mountains

Circle the adjective in each sentence.

Example: I saw a (beautiful) country.

  1. I saw above me that endless skyway.

  2. I saw below me that golden valley.

  3. I saw the sparkling sands.

  4. There were great rivers.

  5. A loud voice was chanting.

Unscramble the sentences. Make sure you use correct word order. Follow the example.

Example: Apache great the hunters were. 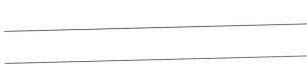 *The Apache were great hunters.*

  6. were they farmers excellent

_____

  7. Navajo warm wove the blankets

_____

  8. the performed special Pueblo ceremonies

_____

  9. carved they images beautiful

_____

_____

  10. climate a Southwest the mild has

_____

_____

SKILLS FOR WRITING

Use with textbook page 19.

Writing Paragraphs

A paragraph is a group of sentences about one idea. Read the sentences below. Think about whether they belong in a paragraph. Ask yourself: Are there any sentences that do not belong? What is the paragraph mainly about? Then follow the directions and answer the questions below.

This Beautiful Land

The United States has many beautiful places to visit.

Don't forget to visit Machu Picchu when you are in Peru.

If you go to California, you can see tall redwood trees and hills covered with golden poppies.

You can climb active volcanoes in Ecuador.

You can swim in the warm waters of the Gulf of Mexico from Texas to Florida.

In the Southwest you'll see large, sandy deserts.

If you like rivers, make sure to see the wide, beautiful Columbia River in the Northwest.

Plan on spending at least a week in Thailand.

When you travel in the Northeast, visit the White Mountains. In winter, you can ski down the slopes.

Wherever you go in the United States, there is something beautiful to see.

1. Write the first sentence that does not belong. _____

2. Write the second sentence that does not belong. _____

3. Is there another sentence that does not belong? If so, write it here.

_____

4. Write the topic sentence. _____

5. What should you do with the first sentence to signal a paragraph? _____

PROOFREADING AND EDITING

Use with textbook page 20.

Read the paragraph carefully. Find all the mistakes. Rewrite the paragraph correctly on the lines below.

Native Americans in America

In school, i learned a lot about Native Americans. the onest thing I learned was they came to this continent many years ago. Some came across a land bridge from asia. she were nomads who moved a lot After many years, native Americans lived in all parts of America We migrated to different parts of what is now the United states. some tribes farmed, and others hunted and fished for food. Some tribes built settlements or cities Others migrated with the animals he hunted for food. Today, we can tell a lot about the lives of people who lived before europeans arrived in this part of the world

_____

_____

_____

_____

_____

_____

_____

_____

_____

_____

_____

_____

_____

SPELLING

Use after the spelling lesson.

Spelling the Long and Short *a* and *e* Sounds

There are many ways to spell words with the vowel sounds short *a*, long *a*, short *e*, and long *e*, but many of these words follow a pattern.

Words with a short *vowel* sound are usually spelled with a *consonant, vowel, consonant* (CVC) pattern:

CVC short *a*:   map   had   land
CVC short *e*:   red   well   men

For words with long *a* and long *e* sounds, look for these letter pairs:

ai	rain	main	painting
ay	way	clay	stay
ee:	teepee	tree	teeth
ea:	meat	steam	bead

Words with the long *a* or *e* sound are also spelled with the CVCe pattern:

CVCe long *a*:   game   whale   made
CVCe long *e*:   these   theme   scene

Read the following words. Circle the words that have the short *a* or *e* sound.

Example: (rest)   please   seeds

1. lay   sand   slave
2. let   feast   tree
3. pass   face   native
4. fail   train   nomad
5. hear   sleeve   west

Circle the words that have the long *a* or *e* sound.

6. stream   stem   let
7. man   plains   saw
8. land   late   calm
9. text   breed   endless
10. play   part   flat

UNIT 1 Journeys of Discovery
PART 2

Contents

VOCABULARY

Use with textbook page 23.

Read each sentence. Then circle the letter next to the word that is closest in meaning to the underlined word.

1. They traveled together on an <u>expedition</u> to the North Pole.

    a. nation   b. trip   c. idea   d. country

2. Because we did not know their language, we needed an <u>interpreter</u> to be able to talk with them.

    a. telephone   b. tribe   c. translator   d. transportation

3. I had seen a picture of my cousin, so I <u>recognized</u> her as soon as I saw her.

    a. knew   b. disliked   c. confused   d. learned

4. I told her that if she didn't like the painting, she could <u>trade</u> it for something else.

    a. hang   b. try   c. take   d. exchange

5. They thought the child had been <u>kidnapped</u> when they couldn't find him, but he was sleeping in the barn.

    a. taken by a stranger   b. sent to camp   c. taken shopping   d. fed

Read the clues. Use the words in the box to complete the crossword puzzle. (Hint: you will not use all of the words, and you will not use any word twice.)

kidnapped	ocean	recognized	trail	moccasins
explorers	trade	interpreter	expedition	mountains

ACROSS
3. large body of water
4. exchange one thing for another
5. long journey

DOWN
1. soft leather shoes
2. captured and taken as a prisoner

VOCABULARY BUILDING

Understanding Prefixes

A **prefix** is a word part that is added at the beginning of a word. Adding a prefix to a word changes the word's meaning. Look at the prefixes and their meanings in the box. Recognizing and knowing the meaning of a prefix can help you figure out a word's meaning.

bi- twice or two	**im-** not	**dis-** opposite of; not

Write the definitions of the words below. Use a dictionary if you need to.

1. bilingual _____

_____

2. impatient _____

_____

3. disapproved _____

_____

4. immovable _____

_____

5. disrespectful _____

_____

Look at the words below. Write each in a sentence. Use a dictionary if you need to.

6. imperfect _____

_____

7. disloyal _____

_____

8. bicycle _____

_____

9. improper _____

_____

10. disadvantage _____

_____

READING STRATEGY

Use with textbook page 23.

Visualizing

Visualizing means that you are creating pictures in your mind. When you read a text, the descriptive words a writer uses can help you visualize.

As you read a text, notice the adjectives and action verbs the writer uses to help you visualize what is happening.

Read the first two paragraphs on page 27 in your textbook. Write three adjectives and two action verbs from the paragraphs.

1. _____

2. _____

3. _____

4. _____

5. _____

Did you form a picture of what the journey was like? Did you form a picture of what the men looked like? List some of your own adjectives and other words to describe the journey and the men below.

6. _____

7. _____

8. _____

9. _____

10. _____

Use with textbook pages 32–34.

Summary: "Reading a Relief Map"

This passage tells how to use a relief map. A **relief map** shows the geographical features of a region, such as plains, hills, and mountains. Different colors on the map show how many meters or feet an area is above sea level. The scale on a map looks like a ruler and shows the distance between places.

Visual Summary

Relief Map
- shows geographical features, including elevation (height)
- has key explaining colors, designs, or other symbols
- shows distances on a scale
- shows sea level as 0 elevation

Name _____ Date _____

Use What You Know

List three things you know about the geography of your area.

1. _____

2. _____

3. _____

Text Structure: Informational Text

An informational text presents factual information to readers. Often it includes definitions or explanations of important terms. Underline the explanation of a relief map in the first paragraph. List three more terms that are explained in the next two paragraphs.

MARK THE TEXT

1. _____

2. _____

3. _____

Reading Strategy: Using Maps

When maps are part of a selection, they will help you understand the selection better. Find the map key. Circle the title that explains what the relief map on page 21 shows. What three countries does the map show?

MARK THE TEXT

_____

_____

_____

Reading a Relief Map

A relief map shows the geographical features of a region. It shows the differences in elevation, or height, of a region. For example, by looking at a relief map, you can see whether the land in a region has plains, hills, or mountains.

Relief maps have a key—a box with different colors, designs, or symbols that tell how high the land is above sea level. Sea level is the level of the surface of the sea where it meets the land. We measure sea level in meters and in feet.

Maps have scales. The scale on a map looks like a ruler. It shows how many kilometers or miles equal a certain distance on the map. You can use the scale to figure out the distance between places on the map.

_____

measure, find the size, weight, or amount of something
distance, amount of space between two places

Choose one and complete:
1. Draw a picture of one of the places discussed in the article.
2. Draw a relief map of your own city or state. Obtain your information from an atlas or the Internet.
3. Describe a job or an activity in which someone might need to use a relief map.

Name _____ Date _____

Western United States, Canada, and Mexico (relief map)

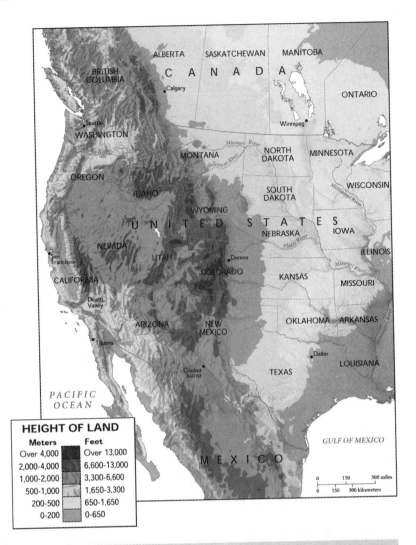

HEIGHT OF LAND

Meters	Feet
Over 4,000	Over 13,000
2,000–4,000	6,600–13,000
1,000–2,000	3,300–6,600
500–1,000	1,650–3,300
200–500	650–1,650
0–200	0–650

Text Structure: Informational Text

An informational text often uses maps and other graphic aids to make the information clear. List two statements from the article that the map helps support or make clear.

1. _____

   _____

   _____

2. _____

   _____

   _____

Reading Strategy: Using Maps

Remember, the colors, designs, or other symbols on a map are usually explained in a box called the key. Circle the key to the map on this page. Based on the key, which state has the most high mountains, Kansas, Colorado, or South Dakota?

_____

Based on the key, write one state that doesn't have any high mountains.

_____

HEIGHT OF LAND

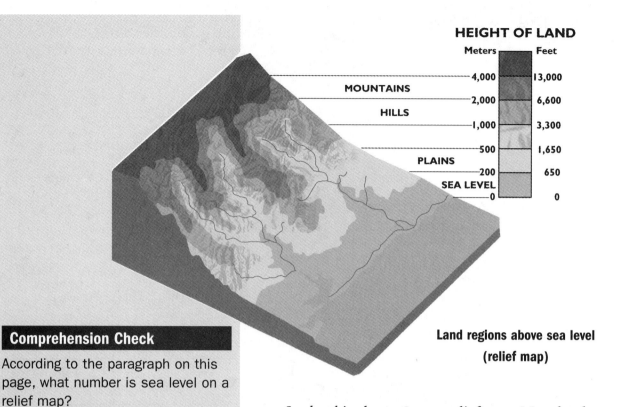

Meters		Feet
4,000		13,000
2,000		6,600
1,000		3,300
500		1,650
200		650
0		0

MOUNTAINS

HILLS

PLAINS

SEA LEVEL

**Land regions above sea level
(relief map)**

Comprehension Check

According to the paragraph on this page, what number is sea level on a relief map?

_____

Circle two American cities mentioned in the paragraph that are partly at sea level.

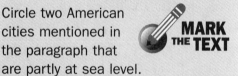

Reading Strategy: Using Maps

Circle and study the key to the map on this page. What name do we give land that is from 200 to 500 meters (650 to 1,650 feet) high?

_____

Which heights are called hills? Which heights are called mountains?

_____

_____

_____

Sea level is always 0 on a relief map. Most land in the United States is above—higher than—sea level. For example, the city of Denver, Colorado, is about 1,609 meters (5,280 feet) above sea level. Dallas, Texas, is about 141 meters (463 feet) above sea level. Cities that are on a seacoast, such as San Francisco, California, and Boston, Massachusetts, have some land that is at sea level and some land that is higher. San Francisco, for example, is about 20 meters (65 feet) above sea level in some places. Some land is below—lower than—sea level. For example, Death Valley in California is 86 meters (282 feet) below sea level.

Retell It!

Make a list of ten things shown on the first map. Or explain, in your own words, all the information shown on the second map.

_____

_____

_____

_____

_____

_____

_____

_____

_____

_____

Reader's Response

How might reading a relief map be useful for you sometime?

_____

_____

_____

_____

Think About the Skill

How did studying and using the maps help you better understand the selection?

_____

_____

_____

_____

_____

GRAMMAR

Use with textbook page 36.

Using the Conjunctions *and* and *or*

A **conjunction** is a word that connects subjects, verbs, or objects in sentences. The words *and* and *or* are conjunctions.

Circle the conjunction in each sentence. Then underline the subjects, verbs, or objects that the conjunctions connect.

1. Meriwether Lewis and William Clark led the expedition.

2. Was Lewis or Clark the stronger leader?

3. They planned and charted a course to the Pacific.

4. Her mother and many others had been killed five winters earlier.

5. The men didn't stop or hunt for food.

Use *and* or *or* to combine each sentence pair below into one sentence.

6. Captain Clark did not study botany. Captain Clark did not study medicine.

   _____

7. They ate buffalo meat. They ate wild berries.

   _____

8. The expedition traveled over plains. The expedition traveled over hills.

   _____

9. The man did not have beads for trade. The man did not have coins for trade.

   _____

10. Sacagawea did not want to live with the Minnetarees. Sacagawea did not want to live with the French-Canadians.

   _____

GRAMMAR

Use after the lesson on parts of speech.

Parts of Speech

There are eight main kinds of words in English, which are called **parts of speech.** Nouns, verbs, and adjectives are examples of parts of speech.

- **Nouns** are the names of people, places, and things.
  Lewis   Missouri   canoes   clothes
- **Verbs** show action or connect the subject to the rest of the sentence.
  tell   is   sit   bring
- **Adjectives** describe nouns.
  white   long   great   treacherous

Read each sentence. Underline the nouns, circle the verbs, and box the adjectives.

Example: White <u>men</u> (came) in [long] boats.

1. Sacagawea carried the little baby.

2. The chief drew a large map.

3. The group saw a small cloud of dust.

4. The men pulled long ropes.

5. Sacagawea wore a heavy blanket.

Each sentence is missing a noun, verb, or adjective. Complete the sentences using words from the box. Follow the example.

sharp	cut	wood	wet	told	explained
was	silent	ran	sang	trip	

Example: Drewyer ____*explained*____ (verb) in sign language.

6. Tears (verb) _____ down her now (adjective) _____ cheeks.

7. The men (verb) _____ their feet on the (adjective) _____ rocks.

8. The soft (noun) _____ under the bark (verb) _____ filling.

9. Charbonneau (verb) _____ Sacagawea about the (noun)

   _____ .

10. She (verb) _____ a/an (adjective) _____ song to the river.

SKILLS FOR WRITING

Use with textbook page 37.

Writing Essays

An **essay** is a group of paragraphs about one topic. All of the information in the essay supports one main idea.

Read the following paragraphs. They are not in the correct order. Decide how the essay should be organized and number the paragraphs from 1 to 5. Then write the details in the space provided.

Sacagawea and the Lewis and Clark Expedition

_____ The group went to the Shoshone camp and spoke with the chief. Sacagawea suddenly knew who he was by his voice and gestures. The chief was her brother, whom she had not seen for five years. Sacagawea had really helped Lewis and Clark. They could now get the horses they needed from the Shoshone.

_____ By midsummer of the expedition, Sacagawea had made an important discovery. She noticed that bark had been stripped away from the pine trees. Her people ate the soft wood underneath when food was scarce. Her people had been in the area. Lewis and Clark had made the right decision.

_____ Lewis and Clark were famous explorers, yet their journey west might not have been possible without the help of a Shoshone woman named Sacagawea. Lewis and Clark did not know the language of the Shoshone and desperately needed to trade with them for horses. They asked Sacagawea to go with them on their expedition. She agreed. She had been kidnapped five years earlier and feared that she might never see her people again. Now she had a chance to find them.

_____ It would be another discovery that would confirm Sacagawea's theory. At the end of one hot day, Sacagawea was now convinced that her people had been in the area. This time, she recognized the white earth on the riverbank. Her people used that earth for paint.

_____ Once they knew the Shoshone were near, thanks to Sacagawea, Captain Lewis and a few others set off to find them. Captain Clark and the others continued their journey up the river. One day, a group of riders were spotted. Sacagawea recognized their clothes and the way they rode horses. Finally, it looked as if they had found the Shoshone.

6. Title: _____

7. Topic: _____

8. Main idea sentence: _____

_____

9. Body paragraphs (list numbers): _____

10. Summary paragraph (list number): _____

PROOFREADING AND EDITING

Use with textbook page 38.

Read the essay carefully. Look for mistakes in capitalization, punctuation, and the use of conjunctions. Find all the mistakes. Then rewrite the essay correctly on the lines below.

William Clark's Map

Before the journey of lewis or clark, maps of North america were not accurate. Mapmakers were not really certain about what the United states looked like. They were familiar with the east coast but not with the land between the mississippi River or the Pacific Ocean

On his expedition, William clark created a map that changed the way people viewed North America. His map was very detailed. It included mountains or rivers. It showed Native american settlements. Most important, it was the first map that connected the eastern or the western United States.

Clark's map of the united States became a road map for travelers. Thousands of settlers used the map to travel to the western United States. The goal President Thomas jefferson had in mind, to open the United States for expansion, became a reality

_____

_____

_____

_____

_____

_____

_____

_____

_____

_____

_____

_____

Name _____ Date _____

SPELLING

Use after the spelling lesson.

Words with Long and Short *i*

There are many ways of spelling the short and long *i* sounds. The chart below shows some of the spelling patterns for the short and long *i* sounds.

Sound	Spelling	Patterns
short *i*	CVC	him, bit
short *i*	CVCC	rich, fish
long *i*	i_e	tribe, ride
long *i*	igh	sigh, night
long *i*	ie	tie, lie
long *i*	y	sky, fly

Circle the words with long *i* sounds.

Example: (find)   dish   fist

1. drink   distant   dry
2. shine   still   sister
3. hill   high   hit
4. since   supplies   sift
5. wife   will   with

Circle the words with short *i* sounds.

6. shine   rib   sight
7. white   while   will
8. fit   fight   file
9. by   bite   dim
10. his   fire   fight

UNIT 2 The Natural World
PART 1

Contents

VOCABULARY

Use with textbook page 49.

Read the paragraph and think about the meaning of the words in **boldfaced** type. Then choose one of the words to complete each sentence. Use a dictionary if needed.

It was amazing how the life forms had managed to live and **interact** with each other in the dry, rocky environment. As with any **ecosystem**, the life forms there were all dependent upon one another for survival. The scientists decided that most of the fossilized animal remains could be labeled **carnivore** because very little plant life could have existed there. However, one of the fossils must have been an **herbivore** because they found only seeds in its digestive tract. In another one, they found bones and stems, and labeled it **omnivore**.

1. An animal that eats both plants and meat is a (an) _____.

2. An animal that eats only meat is called a (an) _____.

3. When two things act upon one another, they _____.

4. An animal that eats only plants is called a (an) _____.

5. A swamp, where every animal is food for another animal, is a (an) _____.

Read the clues. Use the words in the box to complete the crossword puzzle. You will use each word once. Use a dictionary if needed.

| organism | herbivore | interact | ecosystem | omnivore |

ACROSS

3. an animal that eats plants and other animals

4. act upon one another

5. any living thing

DOWN

1. a community of plants and animals dependent upon each other

2. an animal that eats only plants

VOCABULARY BUILDING

Understanding Greek and Latin Roots

Many modern English words come from the ancient Greek and Latin languages. Study the chart below.

L. = Latin Gr. = Greek

Root	English Word
L. populus (the people)	population
L. sumere (use up)	consumers
L. nutrire (nourish)	nutrients
Gr. tropikus (a turn of the sun)	tropical

Root	English Word
L. habitare (dwell)	habitat
L. medius (middle)	medium
L. animas (breath)	animal
Gr. organon (an implement)	organism

Choose a word from the box below to complete each sentence. The box contains words that have Greek or Latin roots from the chart. Use the context of the sentence to choose the word. Write the word on the line.

inhabitants   tropics   nutritious   animated   organs

1. In the movie, the _____ robots moved like living, breathing, real people.

2. The nourishing vitamins in algae make it a _____ source of food for fish.

3. Each of an animal's _____ perform a special function in its body.

4. The _____ of the damaged nest soon left.

5. In the _____, rain forests provide shade from the hot sun.

READING STRATEGY

Use with textbook page 49.

Skimming

Skimming a text means reading it quickly. Skimming can help you get a general understanding of what a text is about. Follow these steps:

- Read the first and second paragraphs quickly.
- Read only the first sentences of the following paragraphs.
- Read the last paragraph quickly.

Turn to pages 50–52 in your textbook. Read the first and second paragraphs quickly to get a general idea of what they are about. Then complete these sentences.

1. The first paragraph tells about _____ .

2. The second paragraph tells about _____ .

Read the first sentence of the next three paragraphs on page 51. Rewrite each one below in your own words.

3. _____

4. _____

5. _____

6. What are the words and definitions listed at the bottom of page 51 about?

_____

Look at the heading on page 52. Skim the two paragraphs.

7. What is meant by "Populations" in the heading? _____

_____

8. What is meant by "Communities" in the heading? _____

_____

Read the last paragraph on textbook page 55 quickly to get a general idea of what it is about.

9. What does the last paragraph tell about? _____ .

_____

10. What do you think this article is mostly about? _____

_____

_____

Use with textbook pages 58–60.

Summary: "The Bat" and "The Snake"

These poems describe two very different animals. "The Bat" tells how a bat looks and flies. "The Snake" tells how a snake moves. Each poet tells what it feels like to come face to face with the animal.

Visual Summaries

The Bat	
By Day	**By Night**
• cousin to mouse	• flies in crazy loops
• lives in an attic	• scary looking
• keeps its wings around its head	• looks like a mouse with wings
• pulse beats very slowly	• face looks human

The Snake
• long and thin
• spotted skin
• likes wet and muddy ground, cold areas, grass
• moves quickly, like a whip
• uncurls in the sun
• inspires fear

The Bat

List three things you know about bats or snakes.

1. _____

2. _____

3. _____

Text Structure: Poem

Poems express emotions, experiences, and ideas. Poems have lines that are often grouped in stanzas. Circle the last stanza of this poem. What emotion do you think this stanza expresses?

MARK THE TEXT

_____

_____

Reading Strategy: Visualizing

Visualizing means picturing something in your mind. Poets often provide details that help you visualize the subject of the poem. Underline three details that help you picture the bat. How is your picture of the bat in the daytime different from your picture of it at night?

MARK THE TEXT

_____

_____

_____

_____

_____

By day the bat is cousin to the mouse.
He likes the attic of an **aging** house.

His fingers make a hat about his head.
His **pulse beat** is so slow we think him dead.

He **loops** in crazy **figures** half the night
Among the trees that face the corner light.

But when he **brushes up** against a **screen**,
We are afraid of what our eyes have seen:

For something is **amiss** or **out of place**
When mice with wings can wear a human face.

Theodore Roethke

_____

aging, becoming older
pulse beat, heartbeat
loops, flies in circles
figures, patterns
brushes up, touches lightly
screen, wire net that covers a window
amiss, wrong
out of place, strange or unusual

The Snake

A narrow fellow in the grass
Occasionally rides;
You may have met him,—did you not,
His notice sudden is.

The grass divides as with a comb,
A spotted shaft is seen;
And then it closes at your feet
And opens further on.

_____

shaft, long, thin object

Choose one and complete:
1. Draw a picture of a bat or a snake based on the description in either poem.
2. Do research in a science book or on the Internet to find out more about bats or snakes. Take notes on the information you find.
3. Hunt for a recording of a piece of music that you think captures the feeling that a bat or snake creates for you. Describe the music you will look for.

Text Structure: Poem

Poets sometimes use unusual word order to keep the rhythm or to capture attention. Underline the words in lines 3 and 4 that appear in unusual order. Restate these words in more usual word order.

MARK THE TEXT

_____

_____

_____

Reading Strategy: Visualizing

Circle three words in the first two stanzas that help you picture the snake. In one sentence, tell what the snake looks like.

MARK THE TEXT

_____

_____

Comprehension Check

Underline the comparison in the second stanza that tells what the snake is doing to the grass. Which of the snake's qualities is stressed in lines 4, 5, 7, and 8?

MARK THE TEXT

_____

_____

_____

Reading Strategy: Visualizing

Underline the details in the poem's fourth stanza that help you picture the snake's movements. What comparison in the stanza helps you picture the snake?

MARK THE TEXT

_____

_____

Literary Element: Rhyme

Two words rhyme if they have the same ending sounds but different beginning sounds. For example, *night* and *light* rhyme. Circle the rhymes in the third, fifth, and sixth stanzas.

MARK THE TEXT

Text Structure: Poem

Underline what happens to the speaker whenever she sees a snake. What overall emotion does the poem convey about snakes?

MARK THE TEXT

_____

_____

He likes a boggy acre,
A floor too cool for corn.
Yet when a child, and barefoot,
I more than once, at morn,

Have passed, I thought, a whip-lash
Unbraiding in the sun—
When, stooping to secure it,
It wrinkled, and was gone.

Several of nature's people
I know, and they know me;
I feel for them a transport
Of cordiality;

But never met this fellow,
Attended or alone,
Without a tighter breathing,
And zero at the bone.

Emily Dickinson

_____

boggy acre, wet and muddy ground
barefoot, without shoes
at morn, in the morning
unbraiding, becoming straight
cordiality, friendliness

Retell It!

Retell either poem as a story about a person seeing a bat or a snake up close. Plan the details of that story here.

_____

_____

_____

_____

_____

_____

Reader's Response

What do you feel about bats or snakes? Why? Express your reaction in a few sentences or a short poem.

_____

_____

_____

_____

_____

_____

_____

_____

Think About the Skill

How did visualizing help you better understand and enjoy the poems?

_____

_____

_____

_____

GRAMMAR

Use with textbook page 62.

Subject-Verb Agreement: Simple Present
In the **simple present**, the subject and verb must agree in number (singular or plural).
This is called **subject-verb agreement.**

Read the rules and examples for subject-verb agreement in this chart.

● Add -s or -es to verbs with singular subjects. A desert <u>snake</u> **needs** shelter from the hot sun.
● Do not add -s or -es to verbs with plural subjects. <u>Plants</u> **use** sunlight and water to make food.
● Do not add -s or -es to verbs with two or more subjects that are combined with *and*. <u>Trout and</u> other freshwater <u>fish</u> **swim** in rivers and lakes.

Put a check mark (✔) on the line next to each sentence in which the subject and verb agree. If the subject and verb do not agree, write the correct spelling of the verb on the line.

1. Many plants and animals live in a rain forest habitat. _____

2. Bats drinks nectar from flowers. _____

3. An eagle snatch fish out of the water. _____

4. Tall trees shade the forest floor. _____

5. Monkeys swing through the trees. _____

6. A fish and a turtle swims in the water. _____

7. The vine wraps around the trees. _____

8. Ants bring pieces of leaves to their nests. _____

9. Snakes slithers along the ground. _____

10. It rain almost every day in a rain forest. _____

GRAMMAR

Use after the lesson about capitalization.

Capitalization

In the English language, the names of specific people and places are **capitalized**. A **capital letter** is also used at the beginning of every sentence and in the main words of titles, such as story and poem titles.

Write the names of specific people and places you know about in the column beneath each heading. Be sure to capitalize correctly. The first examples are done for you.

Specific Person	Specific Place
Emily Dickinson	*New York*
1. _____	5. _____
2. _____	6. _____
3. _____	7. _____
4. _____	8. _____

Underline each letter that should be capitalized.

Example: The <u>w</u>est <u>r</u>idge <u>n</u>ature <u>p</u>reserve is open to the public.

9. many visitors visit this nature preserve to observe animals.

10. kiko fujiama, the author of the story "animals at home," will be visiting there.

11. she is traveling there from her home in sante fe, new mexico.

12. she will be staying in mt. clement while she researches her new book.

13. ms. fujiama is known throughout the east for her stories about nature.

14. did anna like emily dickinson's poem, "the snake"?

15. i read a poem from a book called "the complete works of emily dickinson."

SKILLS FOR WRITING

Use with textbook page 63.

Writing an Expository Paragraph
Expository writing gives factual information to explain something. Read the expository paragraph below and answer the questions.

Animal Survival in the Arctic Region

Animals of the cold Arctic region must survive in their habitat. The polar bear, arctic fox, and arctic hare live there year-round. Thick fur covers their bodies. The few birds that live in the Arctic have feathers that form a thick body cover. The fur and feathers of some animals in the Arctic change. Some animals that are white in the winter turn brown in the summer. This change protects the animals from predators, or other animals that hunt them for food. A thick layer of fat keeps the animals warm. This layer of fat also provides energy when there is not enough food. The offspring of Arctic animals grow quickly during the short summer. Although life is difficult in the Arctic, some species do survive in their cold habitat.

1. How do you know that this is an expository paragraph?

   _____

   _____

2. What is the main idea?

   _____

   _____

3. What is the topic sentence?

   _____

   _____

4. List facts from the paragraph that support the main idea and the topic sentence.

   _____

   _____

   _____

5. Is the last sentence an effective ending sentence? Why or why not?

   _____

   _____

PROOFREADING AND EDITING

Use with textbook page 64.

Read this expository article carefully. Watch for errors in agreement between the subject and simple present verb, capitalization, and spelling. Find the mistakes. Then rewrite the article correctly on the lines below.

The Arctic tundra

The word *tundra* mean "a land without trees." The Arctic tundra cover the area around the North Pole. in the winter, the temperature go as low as –60 degrees Fahrenheit. The winter lasts up to ten months. The temperature rise to 50 degrees during the short summers. Strong winds blows much of the time. there is not much rain.

A layer of ground stay frozen all year. This is known as permafrost. Above the permafrost, a thin layer of soil thaw for a short time in the summer. Small plants can grows then. These plants hugs the ground to stay warm. They bloom quikly. The flowers lasts for six to ten weeks.

_____

_____

_____

_____

_____

_____

_____

_____

_____

_____

SPELLING

Use after the spelling lesson.

Words with Short and Long *o*, Short and Long *u*

Words with the short *o* and short *u* vowel sounds are often spelled with the letters *o* and *u* in the CVC—consonant, vowel, consonant—pattern.

short *o*:   not, mop, rob   short *u*:   pup, rub, fun

Words with the long *o* and *u* sounds can be spelled in different ways. For example, some follow the pattern CVCe—consonant, vowel, consonant, silent e.

long *o*:   bone, mole, pole   long *u*:   tune, mule, lute

Here are some other spellings of long *o* and long *u*.

long *o*:   b<u>oa</u>t, m<u>ow</u>   long *u*:   bl<u>ue</u>, d<u>ew</u>

Read the words below to yourself. Write if the word has the short *o*, long *o*, short *u*, or long *u* sound on the line.

1. mud   _____
2. drop   _____
3. mule   _____
4. sun   _____
5. few   _____
6. pond   _____
7. huge   _____
8. grow   _____
9. run   _____
10. hole   _____
11. boat   _____
12. spot   _____
13. true   _____

14. How many different ways are words with the long *o* sound on this page spelled? Write the different spelling patterns on the line below.

   _____

15. How many different ways are words with the long *u* sound on this page spelled? Write the different spelling patterns on the line below.

   _____

UNIT 2 The Natural World

PART 2

Contents

VOCABULARY

Use with textbook page 67.

Read the paragraphs. Then compare the meaning of the underlined word in each numbered sentence with the meaning of the same word in the paragraphs. Write the letter **A** or **B** on the line to show which paragraph contains the meaning that matches.

A. My grandmother took my little sister Mia and me fishing. We went to her favorite fishing spot along the **bank** of Snow Creek. She showed us how to make our own poles. She used a branch and trimmed off all the **bark**. Then she attached about fifteen feet of **line**. We dug in the soil for **grub** worms. Mia was afraid the grubs would **bite** her finger.

B. The old gold miner worked just below a **line** of aspen trees. He would **grub** for gold about 10 hours everyday until winter came. His world was quiet except for his digging and his loyal little dog's **bark**. When the cold winter wind's **bite** became too harsh, they went down the mountain. He put his little bit of gold in his box at the **bank** every year.

_____ **1.** She knew it was a birch tree by its white bark.

_____ **2.** The fish won't bite because they are getting plenty to eat.

_____ **3.** We formed a line to see the visiting koala at the zoo.

_____ **4.** We watched a wild hog grub in the plant roots for food.

_____ **5.** We walked along the grassy bank of the stream.

_____ **6.** The coyote would bark at the snake and then crouch behind a bush.

_____ **7.** I need to put this money into the bank.

_____ **8.** Colin lifted the rock to find a grub to use for bait.

_____ **9.** The bite of the night air drove the bears back into their cave.

_____ **10.** The raccoon freed its paw from the tangled line.

Read the clues. Use the words in the box to complete the crossword puzzle. (Hint: You will not use all the words.)

| grub | lake | pole | bank | line | bark | game | pile |

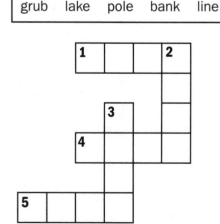

ACROSS
1. wormlike insect
4. raised ground bordering a lake or river
5. string and hook used in fishing

DOWN
2. rough outer covering on a tree
3. animals that are hunted

Unit 2   The Natural World   Part 2

VOCABULARY BUILDING

Understanding Suffixes

A **suffix** is a letter or group of letters added to the end of a word. Knowing the meaning of the suffix and the word it is added to can help you figure out the meaning of the new word. When the suffix begins with a vowel, the silent e ending is usually dropped.

Suffix and its meaning	Word and its meaning	New word with suffix
-ic—having the character of	**athlete**—someone who is active and good at sports	athletic
-y—like	**pine**—a kind of evergreen tree	piney
-ly—in a way	**swift**—fast	swiftly
-able—having the quality of being	**recycle**—to use again and again	recyclable
-ion—the act or condition of	**evaporate**—to become vapor	evaporation

Use the new words in the third column of the chart to complete the following sentences.

1. The two _____ boys climbed the side of the mountain easily.

2. We noticed the _____ smell as soon as we entered the forest.

3. After the rain, the _____ from the plants put moisture in the air.

4. We carried the _____ aluminum cans out of the woods.

5. The strong current moved the boat _____ down the river.

Write the new word formed by adding the suffix. Think about the meaning the adjective gives the noun in *italics*. Remember, silent e is dropped in some words before a suffix.

6. organ + ic = _____ *material*

atmosphere + ic = _____ *conditions*

ocean + ic = _____ *size*

7. frost + y = _____ *ground*

water + y = _____ *habitat*

salt + y = _____ *ocean*

8. excited + ly = _____ *ran*

environmental + ly = _____ *minded*

9. change + able = _____ *liquids*

use + able = _____ *fresh water*

10. distribute + ion = _____ *of land*

condensate + ion = _____ *of liquid*

create + ion = _____ *of gases*

READING STRATEGY

Use with textbook page 67.

Identifying with a Character

You can enjoy and understand what you read when you identify with a character. As you read, ask yourself questions about what the character does and how the character feels. Think about what you would do and how you would feel if you were the character.

Reread pages 68–69 of the excerpt from *My Side of the Mountain* in your textbook. Then answer the questions.

1. What does Sam do after he enters the woods?

_____

_____

2. How does Sam feel?

_____

_____

3. Would I do the same things and feel the same way? Why or why not?

_____

_____

_____

4. Write a sentence explaining how you and Sam are alike.

_____

_____

_____

5. Write a sentence explaining how you and Sam are different.

_____

_____

_____

_____

_____

Unit 2 The Natural World Part 2

Use with textbook pages 76–78.

Summary: "Water and Living Things"

Water is very important to all living things. This passage explains how plants and animals, including people, use water. It also gives information about the different kinds of water found on Earth and explains how water moves from one place to another.

Visual Summary

Cooled in the air, the water vapor condenses into drops that form clouds.

When the water drops get heavy enough, they fall back to Earth as rain.

Heated by the sun, water evaporates into the air.

Water—mostly salt water—covers 3/4 of Earth.

Some of the water is absorbed by the land and by living things. Most of it returns to the sea.

Water and Living Things

Use What You Know

List three things you know about the importance of water.

1._____

2._____

3._____

Text Structure: Expository Nonfiction

Expository nonfiction is writing that explains something. Underline the main idea in the second paragraph. Based on that idea and the title, what do you think this selection explains?

_____

_____

Reading Strategy: Cause and Effect

As you read this article, look for causes and effects. Why is water essential to all living things? Circle the information about how plants use water. How are plants important to animals? What would happen if there were no water?

_____

_____

_____

_____

MARK THE TEXT

What do Earth's surface and human beings have in common? Answer: They both consist mostly of water. Water covers about three-quarters of Earth's surface. Water makes up about two-thirds of the human body. In fact, water is a large part of *every* living thing.

Water is essential for living things to grow, reproduce, and carry out other important life processes. For example, plants use water, plus carbon dioxide and sunlight, to make their food in the process of photosynthesis. Animals and other organisms eat plants or eat other organisms that eat plants. Water is also essential as an environment for living things. Both fresh water and salt water provide habitats for many kinds of living things.

_____

human beings, people
essential, necessary
carry out, complete

Choose one and complete:
1. Draw a poster encouraging people not to waste water and explaining why.
2. Draw a map of the world's oceans. Label the oceans and the continents too. Use an atlas or the Internet to help you with the labels.
3. Write a letter to the editor of a local paper. Explain why fresh water is important, and urge people not to waste it.

Water on Earth

Although Earth has lots of water, the amount of water that humans can use is very small. About 97 percent of Earth's water is the salt water found in the ocean. People have named different parts of the ocean, but in fact these parts are all connected, so they really form a single world ocean.

Only about 3 percent of Earth's water is fresh water. Most of that fresh water is found in the huge **masses** of ice near the North and South Poles. Less than 1 percent of the water on Earth is **available** for humans to use. Some of this available fresh water is found in lakes, rivers, and streams. Other fresh water is located under the ground. This underground water is called groundwater. It fills the small cracks and spaces between underground soil and rocks.

_____

masses, large amounts
available, obtainable; accessible

Comprehension Check

Underline what the first paragraph in "Water on Earth" says about 97 percent of the Earth's water. What kind of water do human beings need?

_____

_____

Text Structure: Expository Nonfiction

Expository nonfiction often uses and defines key terms. Circle a term that is defined on this page. What does the term mean?

_____

_____

_____

Comprehension Check

Underline where most of the fresh water is found. Why do you think most of this water cannot be used?

_____

_____

_____

The Water Cycle

Text Structure: Expository Nonfiction

Expository nonfiction often includes footnotes that define words. Circle the definition of the term *atmosphere*. How do the footnotes define clouds?

MARK THE TEXT

_____

_____

_____

Reading Strategy: Identifying Steps in a Process

Explain in your own words the main steps of the water cycle, in order.

_____

_____

_____

_____

_____

_____

Comprehension Check

What are rain, snow, sleet, and hail an important source of? Underline the words that answer this question. How does Earth's salt water change after it evaporates, condenses, and returns to Earth as precipitation?

MARK THE TEXT

_____

_____

Water is always moving from one place to another. The **continuous** process by which water moves through the living and nonliving parts of the environment is called the water **cycle**. In the water cycle, water moves from bodies of water (such as oceans, rivers, lakes, and streams), land, and living things on Earth's surface to the **atmosphere** and back to Earth's surface.

The sun is the source of energy that creates the water cycle. The sun's energy warms water in oceans, rivers, and lakes. Some of this water evaporates—changes into a gas called water **vapor**. Smaller amounts of water evaporate from the soil, from plants, and from animals (through their skin). Water vapor rises in the air and forms **clouds**. As water vapor cools in the clouds, it condenses, or changes into liquid water drops. When water drops in the clouds become heavy, they fall back to Earth as precipitation—rain, snow, sleet, or hail.

Precipitation is the source of all fresh water on or under Earth's surface. The water cycle renews the supply of **usable** fresh water on Earth.

---

continuous, without stopping
cycle, group of events that happen in the same order over and over
atmosphere, the air that surrounds Earth
vapor, tiny drops of fluid in the air
clouds, tiny drops of water that collect in the air
usable, able to be used

Retell It!

Young children often learn better when they have a character with whom they can identify. Teach the information in this selection by writing a few paragraphs about the life of a drop of water. Tell where the drop travels in the water cycle and why it is important to living things.

_____

_____

_____

_____

_____

_____

_____

_____

_____

_____

Reader's Response

What concerns about fresh water did this selection raise?

_____

_____

_____

_____

Think About the Skill

How did identifying steps in the water cycle and identifying causes and effects help you better understand the selection?

_____

_____

_____

GRAMMAR

Use with textbook page 80.

Using Adverbs to Describe
An **adverb** often describes how an action happens.

- Many adverbs are formed by adding -ly to an adjective.
- An adverb can appear at the beginning or end of a sentence, or before or after the verb.
- **Frequency adverbs** (*always, usually, often, sometimes,* and *never*) come between the subject and the verb.

Read the first sentence with the underlined adjective. Complete the second sentence by forming an adverb from the underlined adjective. Write the adverb on the line.

1. Sam was <u>calm</u> as he sat on the riverbank. Sam _____ sat on the riverbank.

2. It was <u>surprising</u> to hit frozen ground. _____, Sam hit frozen ground.

3. Sam was <u>skillful</u> in making his own hook. Sam _____ made his own hook.

4. With a <u>sudden</u> movement, the string came to life. _____, the string came to life.

5. Sam pulled the string with a <u>powerful</u> jerk. Sam jerked the string _____.

Read the paragraph. Notice the adverbs in italics. Then answer the questions.

Sam used his first fish *wisely*. Because he *sometimes* watched the man in the fish market, Sam knew what to do. The contents of the stomach *always* would tell what the fish were eating. *Frighteningly*, the fish's stomach was empty. Sam *sadly* put some of the internal organs on his hook. He caught five trout *quickly*. Sam gathered firewood *hurriedly*. He tried *desperately* to get a fire going but could not. *Wearily* he crawled into his hemlock tent. He lay *miserably* on his mattress of boughs. He was doing something he *often* thought about but *never* imagined he would do.

_____ **6.** In how many sentences is the adverb at the beginning of the sentence?

_____ **7.** In how many sentences is the adverb immediately before the verb?

_____ **8.** In how many sentences is the adverb immediately after the verb?

_____ **9.** In how many sentences is the adverb at the end of the sentence?

_____ **10.** In how many sentences is a frequency adverb used?

GRAMMAR

Use after the lesson on imperatives.

Imperatives

An **imperative** statement is a statement that directs someone to do something. For example, *Take a camera.* The subject of an imperative sentence is usually not stated directly. It is understood to be *you.*

Rewrite each sentence as an imperative.

1. It is a good idea to take a map when you hike.

_____

2. You should watch for snakes.

_____

3. You must stay on the trail.

_____

4. Will you hand me the fishing pole?

_____

5. You need to use a worm for bait.

_____

6. Will you please wait for me at the lake?

_____

Write an imperative according to each direction.

7. Give directions or instructions.

_____

8. Give a warning.

_____

9. Give an order or a command.

_____

10. Make a polite request.

_____

SKILLS FOR WRITING

Use with textbook page 81.

Describing a Process

When you **describe a process,** the steps must be clear and in correct order. Sequence words help make the order of the steps clear. Read the title and the first sentence of a paragraph below about how to survive in the woods alone. Then read the sentences that follow. Number the sentences from 1-6 to show the order each should be in the paragraph. Then answer the questions. Use signal words to help you.

<u>How to Survive in the Woods Alone</u>

In case you ever become lost in the woods, there are several steps to follow to help you stay safe.

_____ After you find shelter, build a fire, which you can use to keep warm and to signal for help.

_____ First of all, do not panic; stay calm so that you can think clearly.

_____ Then begin to signal for help.

_____ Second, find shelter to protect yourself from the weather and animals.

_____ After you start to signal, cook some food to give yourself energy.

_____ Finally, wait calmly until help arrives.

7. What should you do before you do anything else? _____

8. What should you do before you build a fire? _____

9. When should you cook food? _____

10. Which signal word helped you know what step should be last? _____

PROOFREADING AND EDITING

Use with textbook page 82.

Read the paragraph below carefully. Find the mistakes. Look for mistakes in capitalization, subject-verb agreement, spelling, punctuation, and sequence words. Then rewrite the paragraph correctly on the lines below.

The Importance of fire

Would you know how to survives in the wilderness. The most important skill is the ability to build a fire. You should always has some matchs or a lighter in your backpack. If you get lost in the wilderness, a fire can great help your chances for survival in several ways. Third, if you run out of water, you may have to drink rain or spring water. You will need the fire to boil your water thorough. This will purify it. Second, a fire will keep you warm. First, you can use it to cook your food. Finaly, a fire will keep animals away from your campsite at night.

_____
_____
_____
_____
_____
_____
_____
_____
_____
_____
_____
_____
_____

SPELLING

Use after the spelling lesson.

Adding -ed

Adding *-ed* to a verb tells that an action has already happened. There are different ways to add *-ed*. It depends on how a word is spelled.

The chart below shows the different spelling rules and gives examples of present and simple past tense verbs. Read the rules to add *-ed* and form the simple past.

Rule	Present Tense Verb	Simple Past Verb
For most verbs that end in silent *e*, add *-d*.	breathe	breathed
For most verbs that end in two consonants, add *-ed*.	burn	burned
For most verbs that follow the CVC pattern, double the last consonant and add *-ed*.	cup	cupped
For most verbs that end with a vowel + *w*, *x*, or *y*, do **not** double the consonant. Just add *-ed*.	play	played
For most verbs that end with a consonant + *y*, change the *y* to an *i* and add *-ed*.	cry	cried

Read the paragraph below. Change the present tense verbs in parentheses ( ) into past tense verbs by adding *-ed*. Write the past tense verb on the line. (Hint: Look at the rules in the chart for help!)

I _____ (hike) all day, and then _____ (stop) at the
      1.   **2.**

camping area in the late afternoon. I _____ (want) to start a fire before
                                            3.

dark. I hoped to get it started within a few minutes. I found some wood someone else

had _____ (chop). I _____ (hurry) to light the match. I
     4.   **5.**

_____ (squat) down and blew on the sparks. I felt so excited and so
  6.

lucky. I got the fire going the first time I _____ (try)! I
                                            7.

_____ (smell) the burning wood and _____ (relax). I
  8.   **9.**

took out my carving knife and _____ (whittle) a little fish. I had a
                                10.

wonderful day!

UNIT 3 Striving for Success

PART 1

Contents

VOCABULARY

Use with textbook page 93.

Read each sentence in the first column. Pay attention to the underlined words. Then choose the sentence in the second column that goes with the first sentence. Write the letter of that sentence in the space provided.

_____ **1.** Help me distribute the toys.

_____ **2.** I am reading a good autobiography.

_____ **3.** Our points of view are similar.

_____ **4.** It was an ordinary day.

_____ **5.** We enjoyed a traditional holiday.

a. Nothing unusual happened.

b. We share the same ideas.

c. We practiced the customs we usually do.

d. Be sure everyone gets one.

e. An actor tells his life story in it.

Read the clues. Use the words in the box to complete the crossword puzzle. (Hint: You will not use all the words.)

| information | autobiography | astronaut | evaluate |
| distribute | illustrations | traditional | ordinary |

ACROSS
3. a person who travels into space
4. relating to customs, ideas, and beliefs passed from parents to children

DOWN
1. a book in which the writer tells the story of his or her life
2. give things out
5. average; usual

Unit 3 Striving for Success **Part 1**

VOCABULARY BUILDING

Understanding Suffixes

A **suffix** is a word part that is added to the end of a base word. Together they form another word with a different meaning. The suffixes *-er, -or,* and *-ist* all mean "one who." You can figure out what some words mean if you know the meaning of the suffixes as well as the base words (the word a suffix is added to).

Write the new word that is formed by adding the suffix to the base word below. Then complete the meaning of the new word.

Base Word	Suffix	New Word	Meaning of New Word
paint	*-er*	1. _____	: one who _____
act	*-or*	2. _____	: one who _____
harp	*-ist*	3. _____	: one who plays the _____
teach	*-er*	4. _____	: one who _____
essay	*-ist*	5. _____	: one who writes _____
sail	*-or*	6. _____	: one who _____

Use the words in the box to complete the sentences. (Hint: You will not use all the words.)

dancer	inventor	flutist	writer	player	scientist

7. A(n) _____ is a person who writes.

8. A(n) _____ is a person who dances.

9. A(n) _____ is a person who plays the flute.

10. A(n) _____ is a person who invents things.

READING STRATEGY

Use with textbook page 93.

Making Inferences
Writers don't always give readers every piece of
information. Sometimes readers must infer, or figure out,
what the writer means. This is called **making inferences.**

Read the following statements. Then draw a line under
the sentence that provides the best inference.

1. A famous artist showed her work in New York City,
   Paris, and Mexico City.
   What can you infer about her?

   a. People in cities around the world knew about
      and admired her art.

   b. She was not a well-known painter.

2. A young woman published her first poem when she was seven years old.
   What can you infer about her?

   a. She was a happy child.

   b. She showed a talent for writing at a very young age.

3. After an accident, an actor could not walk. He had to use a wheelchair. However,
   he exercised every day because he believed he would walk again one day.
   What can you infer about him?

   a. He doesn't give up easily.

   b. He is easily discouraged.

4. A computer scientist created the World Wide Web. What can you infer about him?

   a. He must be very intelligent and creative.

   b. He is good at playing games.

5. A 21-year-old art student won a contest to design the Vietnam Veterans Memorial.
   What can you infer about her?

   a. She enjoys painting and drawing.

   b. She is very talented because her work was chosen over others.

Use with textbook pages 102–104.

Summary: "An Interview with Naomi Shihab Nye"

In this interview, poet Naomi Shihab Nye answers an interviewer's questions about her life and her poetry. She tells what it is like to be a writer and when she became interested in poetry.

Visual Summary

Subject	poet Naomi Shihab Nye
Interviewer	Rachel Barenblat
Purpose	to find out about Naomi Shihab Nye and her life as a poet
Audience	young people interested in writing
Main Ideas	Nye has always been curious about the world and interested in poetry. She comes from a multicultural background and has a strong sense of place in her poems. She advises future writers to read and to become part of a circle of writers.

Use What You Know

List three reasons you think someone might decide to become a poet.

1. _____

2. _____

3. _____

Text Structure: Interview

In an interview, an interviewer asks questions that the subject of the interview answers. To find who is interviewing and who is being interviewed, look for the colons (:). Circle the first two colons. Underline the name of the interviewer and the interviewee.

MARK THE TEXT

What is the subject of the interview?

_____

_____

Reading Strategy: Summarizing

Summarizing is retelling just the main ideas. Underline the subject's basic answers to the interviewer's

MARK THE TEXT

questions on this page. Sum up the main idea of the subject's response.

_____

_____

_____

_____

An Interview with Naomi Shihab Nye

Rachel Barenblat

Rachel Barenblat: *When did you start writing? Were you writing poems from the start?*

Naomi Shihab Nye: I started writing when I was six, immediately after learning *how* to write. Yes, I was writing poems from the start. Somehow— from hearing my mother read to me? from looking at books? from watching Carl Sandburg on 1950s black-and-white TV?—I knew what a poem was. I liked the portable, comfortable shape of poems. I liked the space around them and the way you could hold your words at arm's length and look at them. And especially the way they took you to a deeper, quieter place, almost immediately.

Carl Sandburg, famous American poet (1878–1967)
portable, light and easy to carry
comfortable, pleasant and relaxed

Name _____ Date _____

RB: *What did you write about, in the beginning? What provided your first* inspiration*?*

NSN: I wrote about all the little stuff a kid would write about: amazement over things, cats, wounded squirrels found in the street, my friend who moved away, trees, teachers, my funny grandma. At that time I wrote about my German grandma—I wouldn't meet my Palestinian grandma till I was 14.

RB: *Place plays an important role in your writing, especially the places you have lived and the places that hold your* roots*. Tell me about the places that have been important to you.*

NSN: The three main places I have lived— St. Louis, Jerusalem, San Antonio—are each deeply precious to me indeed, and I often find them weaving in and out of my writing. Each place has such distinctive neighborhoods and flavors. . . .

---

inspiration, something that gives you a good idea
amazement, great surprise
roots, connection with a place because you were born there or your family lived there
precious, much loved and very important
distinctive, clearly marking a person or thing as different
flavors, qualities or features

Reading Strategy: Summarizing

Which words in the subject's first response on this page sum up the rest of that response? Underline the words. Circle the details that support it. Sum up the question that this response answers.

MARK THE TEXT

_____
_____

Text Structure: Interview

Sometimes an interviewer makes an observation. Circle the observation that the interviewer makes on this page. How does that observation lead to what she asks the poet to tell about?

MARK THE TEXT

_____
_____
_____
_____

Comprehension Check

Underline the three places where the subject has lived. How does she seem to feel about these places?

MARK THE TEXT

_____
_____

Copyright © 2004 by Pearson Education, Inc.

Unit 3 Striving for Success Part 1   63

Text Structure: Interview

In her questions on this page, where does the interviewer suggest that Nye may do her writing? Underline four places. Explain what the second question on this page shows about the audience at whom the interview is aimed.

MARK THE TEXT

_____

_____

_____

_____

Comprehension Check

Underline the place where Nye says she loves to be. Why is this an unusual place for somebody to write well in?

MARK THE TEXT

_____

_____

_____

Reading Strategy: Summarizing

Underline the advice to future writers that Nye stresses in her final response. Sum up the main points that she makes in this last response.

MARK THE TEXT

_____

_____

_____

RB: *Where do you usually write? Do you have a desk, an office, a favorite chair, a favorite tree?*

NSN: I have a long wooden table where I write. Not a desk, really, as it doesn't have drawers. I wish it had drawers. I can write anywhere. Outside, of course, is always great. I am one of the few people I know who *loves* being in airports. Good thing. I can write and read well in them.

RB: *What is your advice to writers, especially young writers who are just starting out?*

NSN: Number one: Read, read, and then read some more. Always read. Find the voices that speak most to *you*. This is your pleasure and blessing, as well as responsibility!

It is crucial to make one's own writing circle—friends, either close or far, with whom you trade work and discuss it—as a kind of support system, place of conversation and energy. Find those people, even a few, with whom you can share and discuss your works—then do it. Keep the papers flowing among you. Work does not get into the world by itself. We must help it. . . .

_____

pleasure, feeling of happiness or enjoyment
blessing, something that helps you
responsibility, something that you must do
crucial, very important
flowing, moving

Retell It!

Sum up Naomi Shihab Nye's life and achievements in a paragraph that might appear in a reference work about famous poets.

_____

_____

_____

_____

_____

_____

_____

Reader's Response

What did the interview show you about the reasons people choose particular careers or the importance of people's careers in their lives?

_____

_____

_____

_____

_____

Think About the Skill

How did summarizing help you better understand the selection?

_____

_____

_____

_____

GRAMMAR

Use with textbook page 106.

Yes/No and *Wh-* Questions in the Simple Past

- *Yes/no* questions in the simple past usually begin with the word *did* or *didn't*. The main verb is in its base form.

- *Wh-* questions in the simple past begin with a *wh-* word (or *how*) + *did.* The main verb is in its base form.

- When the subject of a *wh-* question is *who* or *what*, a simple past verb follows the *wh-* word.

Circle the correct verb form in parentheses ( ) to complete each question.

1. Who (established / establish) a foundation for people with disabilities?

2. How did Tim Berners-Lee (helped / help) people communicate?

3. What did Mae Jemison (studied / study) in graduate school?

4. When did Frida Kahlo (exhibited / exhibit) paintings in New York?

5. What (change / changed) Maya Lin's life?

Read the statements. Then write a question that the statement answers.

Example: Statement: Maya Lin is an architect.   Question: *Who is Maya Lin?*

6. Statement: Polio weakened Frida Kahlo's right leg.

   Question: _____

7. Statement: Naomi Shihab Nye wrote her first poem when she was seven years old.

   Question: _____

8. Statement: Christopher Reeve did not give up.

   Question: _____

9. Statement: Mae Jemison lived in Chicago as a child.

   Question: _____

10. Statement: Tim Berners-Lee invented the World Wide Web.

    Question: _____

Name _____ Date _____

GRAMMAR

Use after the lesson on *be* verbs in the simple past.

be Verbs in the Simple Past

Verbs in the **simple past** tell about things that have already happened. Simple past forms of the linking verb *be* are *was* and *were*. *Was* is used with a singular subject, except *you*. *Were* is used with a plural subject and *you*. *Were* is always used with the subject *you*.

Read the following interview questions that could be used in interviews with individuals from the selection. Use a *be* verb in the simple past to answer the questions.

1. When did you meet Frida Kahlo? I met her when

   she _____ an art student.

2. How old were you when you published your first poem? I _____ seven years old.

3. What graduate courses did you take? My courses _____ in engineering.

4. What were you most famous for? I _____ well-known for my role in *Superman*.

5. Who were the people in Frida Kahlo's portraits? They _____ her friends.

6. Who did your memorial honor? It honored men and women who

   _____ in the Vietnam War and who fought and died in it.

7. What happened to you in 1995? I _____ in a horseback riding accident.

8. What happened to you and fourteen others in 1987? We _____ the fifteen people out of 2,000 to be selected for NASA's astronaut training program.

9. What was the Internet before your invention of the Web? It _____ a collection of computers that contained lots of information.

10. What were some of your other projects? They _____ a sculpture, a clock, and a Civil Rights memorial.

SKILLS FOR WRITING

Use with textbook page 107.

Writing Narratives: Interview Questions

Before writing narratives about people, writers often interview them. To find out information, most writers use interview questions with *wh-* words. Writers may ask about:

- *where* the person lives
- *who* inspired him or her
- *why* he or she did something
- *when* something important happened
- *what* he or she did
- *how* he or she did it

Complete the questions below for an interview with Tim Berners-Lee. Choose a word from the box. Read the clues in parentheses ( ) to help you complete each question.

Who   What   When   Where   Why   How

1. (place) _____ did you go to college?

2. (which) _____ occupation did you choose?

3. (person) _____ inspired you to become a computer scientist?

4. (in what way) _____ and (time) _____ did you think of your invention?

5. (for what reason) _____ did you want to invent the Web?

Write five questions you would ask in an interview with writer Naomi Shihab Nye. Use *wh-* words from the box above.

6. _____

7. _____

8. _____

9. _____

10. _____

PROOFREADING AND EDITING

Use with textbook page 108.

Read the following interview carefully. Find the mistakes. There are mistakes in forming questions, spelling, capitalization, and punctuation. Then rewrite the interview correctly on the lines below.

An Interview with Dressmaker Tilly Johansen

Interviewer: *Tilly, you are a sucess story in many ways. Didn't you come to America from another country*

Tilly: Yes, my family came to this country from sweden. I was just ten years old. My father was farmer in michigan. That's where I start my sowing business.

Interviewer: *Who did helped you start your busness?*

Tilly: No one helped me. I do it on my own when I be just a teenager!

Interviewer: *What did you make money?*

Tilly: I made money by sewing dresses. I gave most of the money to my family. I saved some for Myself, too

Interviewer: *Did you go to school while you were working?*

Tilly: Yes, I did. i loved school and learned english very quickly. I had a good teacher.

_____

_____

_____

_____

_____

_____

_____

_____

_____

_____

_____

_____

_____

_____

Name _____ Date _____

Occupation Words

The suffixes *-or, -er,* or *-ist* mean "one who" when added to the end of a base word. Many occupation or job names are formed by adding *-er, -or* or *-ist* to a base word.

Base Word	Suffix	Occupation Word
garden +	*-er*	gardener
sculpt +	*-or*	sculptor

Words that end in an *e* will drop the *e* before adding the suffix.

Drop *e* in Base Word	Suffix	Occupation Word
write +	*-er*	writer
type +	*-ist*	typist

Fill in the chart. Add *-er, -or,* or *-ist* to the base word to form an occupation word. Write the new word and complete its meaning.

Base Word + Suffix	New Word	Meaning
1. sing + *-er*		One who _____
2. act + *-or*		One who _____
3. art + *-ist*		One who creates _____
4. design + *-er*		One who _____
5. navigate + *-or*		One who _____
6. drive + *-er*		One who _____
7. sail + *-or*		One who _____
8. report + *-er*		One who _____
9. invent + *-or*		One who _____
10. organ + *-ist*		One who plays _____

UNIT 3 Striving for Success
PART 2

Contents

VOCABULARY

Use with textbook page 111.

Complete each sentence. Use the words in the box. You will not use all of the words.

| bells | coincidence | ground | package | seeds | wilt |

1. If you don't put flowers in water, they will _____.

2. Adrian planted sunflower _____ in her yard.

3. Douglas didn't eat his ice cream cone because it fell on the _____.

4. When Lin dropped her books in front of Phil, it was not a _____.

5. Belinda unwrapped her birthday _____ as soon as it was delivered.

Read the clues. Use the words in the word box to complete the crossword puzzle. (Hint: You will not use all the words.)

| ground | garden | seeds | plantation | grow |
| vegetables | wilt | porch | passengers | pick |

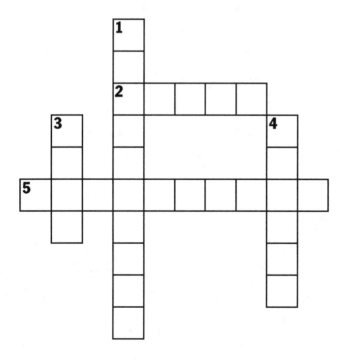

ACROSS

2. the parts of flowering plants from which new plants can grow

5. a large farm, especially in warm climates, where crops, such as cotton, coffee, or sugar, are grown

DOWN

1. people traveling in, but not driving, a vehicle

3. droop

4. the soil on the surface of the earth

Name _____ Date _____

VOCABULARY BUILDING

Understanding Similes

A **simile** describes one thing by comparing it with something else. A simile uses the word *like* or *as*.

Read the sentences below. The author of the selection from *Seedfolks*—the story you will read next—uses similes to tell about a lettuce garden that a boy named Virgil and his father are trying to grow. Find the simile and underline the word *like* in each. In one case, there are two similes, so you will underline *like* twice. Then tell what is being compared.

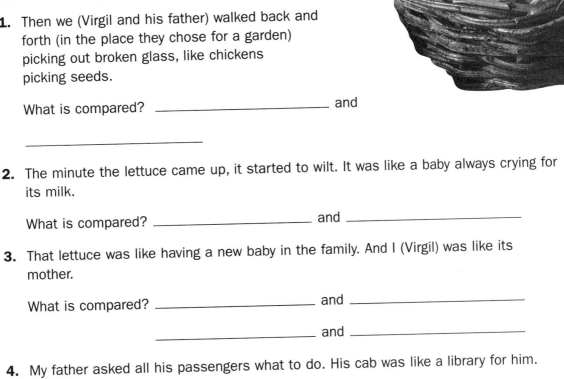

1. Then we (Virgil and his father) walked back and forth (in the place they chose for a garden) picking out broken glass, like chickens picking seeds.

   What is compared? _____ and

   _____

2. The minute the lettuce came up, it started to wilt. It was like a baby always crying for its milk.

   What is compared? _____ and _____

3. That lettuce was like having a new baby in the family. And I (Virgil) was like its mother.

   What is compared? _____ and _____

   _____ and _____

4. My father asked all his passengers what to do. His cab was like a library for him.

   What is compared? _____ and _____

5. In our book, the goddess of crops and the earth had a sad mouth and flowers around her, just like the girl in the locket . . . Then I (Virgil) whispered: "Save our lettuce."

   What is compared? _____ and _____

READING STRATEGY

Use with textbook page 111.

Monitoring Comprehension

As you read, it helps to **monitor your comprehension,** or check your understanding of the text. To do this, stop at certain points in your reading. Try to paraphrase, or tell in your own words, what you just read. Then write any questions you have about what you just read. You may have questions about:

- words or phrases you don't understand
- something that happens in the story that doesn't make sense
- who the characters are
- where the story takes place

Read the following paragraph. Then write what happened in your own words on the lines below.

Janna had one goal. That was to have the best garden in Sommerville. She had planted tomatoes, corn, and carrots in early May. Then disaster struck. A terrible storm beat down all her tiny plants. After that, there was only a slim chance that she would win the prize for Best Teen Garden. Then the solution to her problem finally dawned on her. She would start over with seedlings from the nursery. There was a slim chance that she might still win.

1. _____

_____

_____

_____

_____

_____

Write four questions you have about the paragraph you just read.

2. _____

3. _____

4. _____

5. _____

Use with textbook pages 120–122.

Summary: "How Seeds and Plants Grow"

This passage explains the parts of a seed and the changes a seed goes through to become a plant. Seeds contain almost everything they will need to develop. When the time is right, the seed begins to grow. When the stem and first leaves are above ground, sunlight helps the young plant make its own food.

Visual Summary

(1) A seed has an embryo with **(a)** the basic parts that develop into a plant; **(b)** stored food to feed the plant; and **(c)** an outer covering called the seed coat.

(2) During germination, the seed absorbs water, the seed coat breaks open, and the roots grow downward.

(3) Then the stem and leaves break out and begin growing upward.

How Seeds and Plants Grow

Parts of a Seed

Most plants produce new plants from seeds. A seed is like a tiny package. It contains the beginning of a very young plant inside a **protective** covering.

A seed has three important parts—an embryo, stored food, and a seed coat. The embryo contains the basic parts from which a young plant will develop—**roots**, **stems**, and **leaves**. Stored food keeps the young plant alive until it can make its own food through photosynthesis. Seeds contain one or two seed leaves, called cotyledons. In some plants, food is stored in the cotyledons.

---

protective, concerned with keeping something safe from danger
roots, parts of plants that grow underground
stems, long, thin parts of plants from which leaves or flowers grow
leaves, flat, green parts of plants that grow from branches or stems

Copyright © 2004 by Pearson Education, Inc.

Use What You Know

List three things you know about how plants grow.

1._____
2._____
3._____

Text Structure: Informational Text

An informational text presents factual information to readers. Often it includes definitions or explanations of important terms. Circle two key terms that are explained on this page. Explain what each term is.

MARK THE TEXT

_____

_____

Reading Strategy: Monitoring Comprehension

When you monitor comprehension, you check how well you are understanding what you read. One way to do that is to ask questions and see if you can answer them. Questions you create from titles and headings (usually in **boldfaced type**) are often very useful. Circle the title and heading on this page. What would you ask based on this title and heading? Write your question and answer it.

MARK THE TEXT

_____

_____

_____

The outer protective covering of a seed is called the seed coat. The seed coat is like a plastic wrap, which protects the embryo and stored food from drying out. This protection is necessary because a seed may be inactive—may not begin to grow—for weeks, months, or even years. Then, when conditions are right, the embryo inside a seed suddenly becomes active and begins to grow. The time when the embryo first begins to grow is called germination.

Choose one and complete:
1. Draw some quick sketches of the stages of germination.
2. How can you tell when a seed has germinated? Do research on the Internet or in gardening manuals to find out more about what different seeds look like when they germinate and begin growing leaves. Take notes on the information.
3. Imagine that you are explaining how seeds and plants grow. What details would you include in your spoken explanation? List your ideas.

Text Structure: Informational Text

Underline the definition of a seed coat. How does the comparison to plastic wrap help the reader understand what a seed coat does?

_____

_____

_____

Comprehension Check

Circle the word that describes a seed that does not grow. What new conditions do you think might make a seed begin to grow?

_____

_____

_____

_____

Reading Strategy: Monitoring Comprehension

Remember, asking and answering questions can help you monitor comprehension. What questions might you ask about this paragraph? List two.

_____

_____

_____

_____

_____

Germination

During germination, the seed **absorbs** water from the environment. Then the embryo uses its stored food to begin to grow. The seed coat breaks open, and the embryo's roots grow **downward**. Then its stem and leaves grow **upward**. As the stem grows longer, it breaks out of the ground. **Once** it is above the ground, the stem **straightens** up toward the sunlight, and the first leaves appear on the stem. When the young plant produces its first leaves, it can begin to make its own food by photosynthesis.

---

absorbs, takes in water slowly
downward, from a higher place to a lower place
upward, from a lower place to a higher place
once, when
straightens, becomes free of curves and bends

Reading Strategy: Monitoring Comprehension

Circle the heading for this section. Then create a question based on the heading. **MARK THE TEXT**

_____

_____

_____

_____

_____

_____

Comprehension Check

What substance must the seed absorb in order to germinate, or start growing? Underline the answer. Where do you think this substance comes from? Guess two possible sources. **MARK THE TEXT**

_____

_____

Comprehension Check

Circle the part of the plant that grows first and the parts that grow second, and number them *1* and *2*. How does the plant get its food at first, and how does it get food later? **MARK THE TEXT**

_____

_____

_____

Choose one and complete:
1. Imagine that you work for a TV science show and are filming a seed growing. What music would you use in the background? Describe your ideas.
2. Do research on the Internet or in gardening manuals to find out how to plant and grow a particular kind of seed. Then write a set of instructions for growing that kind of seed.
3. Create a very short story about the adventures of a seed. The story will be told out loud to a group of young children.

Retell It!

Imagine you write for the science section of a local newspaper. Write a short summary of an article you plan to write on plant growth. Use details from the article you just read.

_____

_____

_____

_____

_____

_____

_____

Reader's Response

What did this article show you about nature and the way it works?

_____

_____

_____

_____

_____

Think About the Skill

How did your understanding of the article improve when you monitored comprehension by asking and answering questions?

_____

_____

_____

_____

GRAMMAR

Use with textbook page 124.

Using Compound Sentences

- A **compound sentence** has two or more **independent clauses** joined by a **coordinating conjunction**—*and, but, so, for,* and *or.*
- An independent clause is a complete sentence. It has a subject and a verb.
- Each of the coordinating conjunctions has a different purpose. A comma comes after the first independent clause.

Study the purpose of each coordinating conjunction. Notice the placement of the comma.

Coordinating Conjunction	Purpose
and—He pulled out the weeds, **and** he picked roses.	to add
for—We wore coats, **for** it was very chilly.	to tell why (cause)
but—I like doing yard work, **but** it is tiring.	to contrast
or—You can rake, **or** you can dig.	to show choice
so—The melon was ready, **so** we picked it.	to tell an effect

Circle the coordinating conjunction in each sentence. In the space provided, write the purpose of the coordinating conjunction in the sentence.

Example: _to contrast_   We can plant the seeds in July, (but) they may not germinate.

_____ **1.** Anna turned the soil, and Tom helped her plant the seeds.

_____ **2.** The ground was very hard, so they used a large shovel.

_____ **3.** Digging in the sun was hot work, but they didn't give up.

_____ **4.** Diego didn't offer to help them, for he wasn't interested in gardening.

_____ **5.** Anna watered the plants, and Tom pulled out the weeds.

_____ **6.** She poured the water a little at a time, so the seeds wouldn't be washed away.

_____ **7.** Their garden could be a great success, or it could be a failure.

_____ **8.** Anna did not worry about the garden, for plants are easy to grow.

_____ **9.** Mrs. Sanchez came to visit them, but she didn't stay long.

_____ **10.** The sky was clear in the morning, but by afternoon a light rain began to fall.

GRAMMAR

Use after the lesson on negative past sentences.

Negative Past Sentences

Verbs in the simple past can be written in the affirmative or in the negative. To write a **negative simple past sentence**, use *did* + *not* + the base form of the verb.

For example: **Affirmative:**   I **played** soccer on Saturday
               Negative: I **did not play** soccer on Saturday.

Rewrite the affirmative sentences below as negative past sentences.

1. The lettuce grew quickly.

_____

2. We weeded the garden today.

_____

3. The leaves turned yellow.

_____

4. I saw Miss Fleck coming toward us.

_____

5. The flowers bloomed in July.

_____

6. The gardener needed a lot of help.

_____

7. I helped with the garden today.

_____

8. My neighbor weeded his garden all week.

_____

9. We watched for insects on the leaves.

_____

10. Katie watered the flowers on Monday.

_____

SKILLS FOR WRITING

Use with textbook page 125.

Writing a Personal Narrative

In a **personal narrative**, the writer tells about his or her own experiences and may express personal opinions and feelings. A personal narrative uses the first-person point of view and personal pronouns such as *I, we, me, my, mine, us, our,* and *ours.*

Read the personal narrative below. Then answer the questions.

My Bat House

I am so proud of the bat house I built with my father last spring. Our house is near a lake, so there are lots of mosquitoes. We can't walk in the yard without being bitten!

One day I was reading about bats, and I learned that they could actually help us solve this problem! I read in my encyclopedia that they can eat as much as their own weight in mosquitoes in one night! Many people think bats are ugly and scary, but I like them because they are actually helpful creatures.

I asked my dad to help me build a bat house to attract bats to our backyard. The bat house we built is similar to a birdhouse. We drew a plan, cut out the plywood and wire mesh, and nailed it all together. We made it big enough for forty bats. Dad mounted it on a pole. Since the bats have come to live in our bat house, the mosquito problem has gotten a lot better.

Our bat house has been a real success. We can enjoy being outside without being attacked by mosquitoes. It has been so successful, in fact, that we are helping our neighbor build his own bat house.

1. What is the title of the personal narrative?

_____

2. What personal pronouns tell you the author is using the first-person point of view?

_____

3. What are some personal opinions the writer expresses?

_____

_____

4. What personal experience did the writer and his dad share?

_____

5. What are some words that show the author's feelings about his subject?

_____

PROOFREADING AND EDITING

Use with textbook page 126.

Read this personal narrative carefully. Find the mistakes. Be sure that first-person pronouns are used where they should be used. In addition, check whether the correct form of the pronoun is used. Also look for mistakes in capitalization, verb form, and punctuation. Combine sentences with coordinating conjunctions as needed. Then rewrite the personal narrative correctly on the lines below.

My Favorite garden

our class gone on a trip to the Chandler Botanical Gardens. We seen several sections of the gardens. I liked the english Garden, but mine favorite was the asian bonsai section. The guide said the italian sections were'nt open. They were being redesigned. It will take lots of time and money. but the finished sight will be worth the effort.

Bonsai plants are miniature plants that look like tiny trees. Growing bonsai plants is'nt easy But, some people enjoy it. Gardeners uses special tools to cut the little plants. they must cut the plants at certain places. Or the plants won't grow in interesting shapes.

There is a lot to see at the gardens so, I hope to go again soon.

_____

_____

_____

_____

_____

_____

_____

_____

_____

_____

SPELLING

Use after the spelling lesson.

Initial *w* and *j*

Many words begin with the sound you hear at the beginning of the word *want*. These words are spelled with the letter *w*.

For example:

was   watering   weekend

Many other words begin with the sound you hear at the beginning of the word *June*. These words are often spelled with the letter *j*.

For example:

just   jacket   jam

Read the sentences below. Circle the word in parentheses (with initial *w* or *j*) that correctly completes each sentence.

1. That night he drove himself (way / jay) across town to borrow two shovels from a friend of his.

2. School was over, but that garden was (just / worst) starting.

3. I hardly recognized her in (weans / jeans).

4. He tried to show me something when I poured out the (water / jogger).

5. The minute it came up, it started to (jilt / wilt).

6. She pronounced every letter in every (word / jar).

7. My eyes opened (jarred / wide).

8. This one is for my (wife's / jeep's) father.

9. Then I opened it up (was / just) a crack.

10. The lettuce finally came up in (jacket / wavy) lines.

UNIT 4 Change

PART 1

Contents

VOCABULARY

Use with textbook page 137.

Use the context to figure out the meaning of the underlined word. Then use the word to answer the question.

1. Computers, telephones, and televisions use <u>technologies</u> that make our lives easier. What other <u>technologies</u> in your home make your life easier?

_____

2. When we <u>waste</u> money, we spend it on things that are unnecessary. What is something else that people <u>waste</u>?

_____

3. Different <u>chemicals</u> help us clean our ovens, kill insect pests, and even soften fabrics. What are two products you know that use <u>chemicals</u>?

_____

4. Factories and cars burn gasoline and oil, which causes air <u>pollution</u>. What causes

water <u>pollution</u>? _____

5. <u>Nuclear power</u> is released when an atom's nucleus splits. What is one use of

nuclear power? _____

6. We must protect Earth's natural <u>resources</u>, such as its water, land, gas, and oil. What is being done to protect natural <u>resources</u>?

_____

Read the clues. Use the words in the box to complete the crossword puzzle. (Hint: You will not use all the words, and you will not use any word twice.)

| resources   waste   survive   safer   chemicals   changes   nuclear   pollution |

ACROSS
3. These substances help us do many things, but they can be harmful, too.
4. These are found in nature and are useful or necessary to people. Water is one.

DOWN
1. There are many of these power plants.
2. To use something in a careless way

VOCABULARY BUILDING

Understanding Phrasal Verbs

A **phrasal verb** is a verb that is followed by an adverb or a preposition. Some phrasal verbs are followed by both an adverb and a preposition. An example is *look forward to*. When the words are combined, they form an expression. The meaning of the phrasal verb is different from the meaning of the verb *look* by itself.

Look at the chart.

Verb	Meaning	Phrasal Verb	Meaning
keep	to have something and not get rid of it	keep up (with something or someone)	stay even; prevent from going to a lower level
run	to move or make something move quickly; to operate or function; to flow	run out (of something)	use up; finish the supply of something
runs	moves or makes something move quickly; operates or functions; flows	runs off	drains away; flows away

Read the following sentences. Rewrite each one using a word or phrase to replace the underlined phrasal verb. Use context to figure out the meanings of the phrasal verbs.

Example:

<u>Cut down on</u> your use of water by taking shorter showers.

Reduce your use of water by taking shorter showers. _____

1. <u>Turn off</u> the lights when you leave a room. _____

_____

2. Don't <u>throw away</u> things that can be used again. _____

_____

3. <u>Put off</u> doing laundry until you have enough to fill your washing machine.

_____

4. <u>Cut back</u> on use of products that contain chemicals. _____

_____

5. Use a cloth shopping bag that won't <u>wear out</u> as quickly as a paper or plastic one.

_____

READING STRATEGY

Use with textbook page 137.

Noting Causes, Effects, and Solutions
Science texts often have a **cause-and-effect organization**. When you read science articles, such as "Changing Earth" on pages 138–143 in your textbook, look for causes and effects.

- Look for words that signal a cause, such as *because of, as a result of,* and *results from*.
- Look for words that signal an effect, such as *so, therefore,* and *causes*.
- Read carefully to understand relationships between causes, effects, and solutions.

Read the following sentences. Decide whether the underlined sentence or part of a sentence is a cause or an effect, and write it in the correct column of the chart.

1. <u>Because this is such a new technology,</u> scientists are not yet sure how genetically engineered plants and animals will affect other living things.

2. The number of people on Earth is growing, <u>so the need for energy, food, and water is growing</u>.

3. Sunlight varies with the weather and the time of day. <u>Therefore, solar power is not always available to generate electricity</u>.

4. People did not know that burning fossil fuels could affect the environment, <u>so they used them as an energy source</u>.

5. <u>As a result of food shortages,</u> scientists have looked for ways to make plants more productive.

Cause	Effect

Use with textbook pages 146–148.

Summary: "The Intersection"

This selection consists of three fictional letters to a newspaper. The letters all describe problems at one intersection. They were written fifty years apart, in 1900, 1950, and 2000, by a grandfather, father, and son in the same family. In each letter, the writer—Jason Winthrop, Jason Winthrop Jr., or Jason Winthrop III— asks people to change the way they drive to prevent accidents and reduce noise at the intersection.

Visual Summary

Year	Writer	Travel Means	Main and Third	Downtown	Request
1900	Jason Winthrop	horses, carriages, early cars	dirt	some homes and offices	go slow
1950	Jason Winthrop Jr.	cars, trolleys, buses	paved, two-way, traffic light	many homes and offices	go slow, stop blowing horn
2000	Jason Winthrop III	mostly cars, no trolleys	paved, one-way	many offices and parking lots, just one home	go slow

Use What You Know

Write what you know about the history of transportation in cities.

_____

_____

_____

Text Structure: Persuasive Letter

People with opinions on local and other issues often express them in letters to newspapers, on TV stations, and in other media. They often try to persuade others to help support their viewpoint. Underline the address of the person who wrote

MARK THE TEXT

this persuasive letter and the date of the letter. Though the letter is addressed to the editor of a newspaper, who does the writer really want to read the letter?

_____

_____

_____

Reading Strategy: Comparing and Contrasting

Circle the comparison the writer makes between horse-drawn carriages and motor cars. What does the writer fear will happen as the new cars become more widely used?

_____

_____

The Intersection

Dina Anastasio

52 Main Street
January 2, 1900
To the Editor:

I am writing this letter to ask your readers for help. I live on the corner of Main and Third Streets. When it rains, this dirt road turns to mud. When it snows, it turns to slush.

From my sitting room window I see carriages race through the intersection. They are going too fast for such a slippery corner. The drivers do not look where they are going. Often another carriage is coming the other way. The horses rear up. The carriages turn over. Too many people are hurt.

Last night, I helped to pull a horse out of the mud again. The carriage had turned over. A woman broke her leg.

We have now moved into the twentieth century. The horseless carriage is about to change our lives. I hear that Mr. Henry Ford is trying to develop one right now. These motor cars will move people faster than we can imagine. Everyone says that they will solve all our traffic problems. But I'm not sure how. They will race past my house from morning to night. If we aren't careful, they will bang into each other on this corner. They will disturb my sleep. . . .

So please try and drive a little slower when you come to the corner of Main and Third.

Yours sincerely,
Jason Winthrop

---

intersection, place where two roads or streets cross
slush, partly melted snow
carriages, vehicles that horses pull
rear up, rise on back legs

52 Main Street
January 2, 1950
To the Editor:

Fifty years ago, my father wrote to your newspaper. He asked for his neighbors' help. At that time he was **concerned** about speeding. He was worried about the mud and slush on the road. He wanted people to slow down their horses and carriages.

Since that time, our city has changed. There are now 100,000 people instead of 10,000. Electric lights have replaced gas lights. Houses have been pulled down. Apartment and office buildings have replaced them.

I have watched these changes from my living room window ever since I was a child. I watched workers cover the road in front of my house with cobblestones. And after that I watched them pave it. I remember the day the first stop sign was put up on our corner.

I also remember the day, in 1929, when the first electric traffic light went up. Those lights were needed. Motor cars came speeding by, and they needed to be controlled.

This city is still getting larger. More and more people are moving here. That will mean more and more cars. Although there are **trolleys** and buses today, traffic is still a problem.

I cannot stop all the accidents. But I would like to stop the accidents that happen on my corner. And that is one reason that I am writing this letter.

Please slow down! I am tired of **dragging** injured people out of their cars.

I am writing for another reason, too. Cars are polluting our city. There may be nothing that we can do about our polluted air. But there is something that we can do about the noise.

So please stop blowing your horns! I need my sleep!

> Best wishes,
> Jason Winthrop Jr.

---

concerned, worried
trolleys, vehicles that use tracks and are powered by electric current from overhead wires
dragging, pulling

Unit 4 Change Part 1

Comprehension Check

Underline the date of this letter and the relationship of the writer to the person who wrote the first letter. Where does the current writer live?

_____

_____

Reading Strategy: Comparing and Contrasting

Circle four changes that have taken place since the 1900 letter. What are some things that have stayed the same?

_____

_____

_____

Text Structure: Persuasive Letter

Persuasive letters that state problems often end with a request for action that the writer thinks will solve the problem. Underline two problems that the writer of this letter complains about. What two requests does he make?

_____

_____

_____

Text Structure: Persuasive Letter

This persuasive letter opens with the writer restating requests made by his grandfather and father in past letters to the same newspaper. Underline those requests. How does including this background information help make the letter more effective and persuasive?

MARK THE TEXT

_____

_____

_____

Comprehension Check

Circle details in the second paragraph that describe the writer's neighborhood. Why do you think the writer has refused to sell the house?

MARK THE TEXT

_____

_____

_____

Reading Strategy: Comparing and Contrasting

Underline three changes mentioned in the fourth paragraph. Even with these changes, why is traffic outside still a problem for the writer?

MARK THE TEXT

_____

_____

_____

52 Main Street
January 2, 2000
To the Editor:

One hundred years ago today, my grandfather wrote a letter to this newspaper. He asked your readers to slow down when they came to the corner of Main Street and Third. Fifty years later, my father wrote a letter, too. He asked your readers to slow down and stop blowing their horns.

Today, I too am asking for help. Our family still lives in the same house, and I have watched our city change over the past fifty years. This is now a big city. All around me are office buildings and parking lots. My home is the only house left in the whole downtown. Many people have begged me to sell it. But I will not sell.

This is not a fancy house. It is a small wooden house. It is not worth the money that people have offered me. But I do not care about the money. My family has lived here for over one hundred years. I hope we will live here for another hundred.

I would like to tell you what I see from my window. In some ways, the view is the same as my grandfather's view. I still see some of the things that my father saw, too. We have all seen traffic problems. Today, our street has been paved many times. The trolleys are gone. Traffic lights are now run by computers. Best of all, our street is now one-way.

Everyone said that a one-way street would cut the number of accidents in half. But it didn't.

People drive faster because it is one-way. Sometimes they even drag-race here. Beating the light is too often a game. So there are still accidents. People still get very badly hurt, because they go faster. . . .

So my family asks you again, for the third time, to slow down.

Sincerely,
Jason Winthrop III

---

begged, asked in an anxious way
fancy, elaborate and often expensive
drag-race, race from a standstill to a fast speed
beating the light, driving quickly through an intersection just as the traffic light turns red

Retell It!

Choose one of the letters. As the editor of the newspaper, sum up the letter and write a reply. Do you agree with the writer? Tell why or why not.

_____

_____

_____

_____

_____

_____

_____

Reader's Response

What did you find especially interesting or amusing about "The Intersection"?

_____

_____

_____

_____

_____

_____

_____

Think About the Skill

How did comparing and contrasting help you better understand and appreciate the letters?

_____

_____

_____

_____

GRAMMAR

Use with textbook page 150.

Real Conditionals: Sentences with *if*

Real conditional sentences include a main clause and an *if* clause. The *if* clause tells a condition that may or may not happen. The main clause tells the result or possible result of that condition. The verb form used in the main clause depends on whether the conditional event is one that *usually* happens or one that *might* happen in the future.

	if Clause	Main Clause	Example
Events that usually happen	Use a simple present verb.	Use a simple present verb.	If a car **gets** low mileage, it **uses** more gasoline.
Events that might happen in the future	Use a simple present verb.	Use a simple future verb.	If we **plant** carefully, we **will have** a good strawberry crop this year.

Read each sentence. Write the verb in parentheses ( ) in the simple present or simple future form.

1. If a farmer uses fertilizers, he (add) _____ nutrients to the soil.

2. The plants (grow) _____ better if we kill all the weeds.

3. If scientists figure out a way to use genetic engineering, the world's food supply

(increase) _____ .

4. If the battery dies, the car (stop) _____ .

5. An accident (happen) _____ if a nuclear plant fails for some reason.

Match the clause in Column A with the clause in Column B to form a sentence. Write the letter for the matching clause in the space provided.

Column A	Column B
_____ **6.** If farmers grow bigger, stronger crops,	**a.** if we drive hybrid cars.
_____ **7.** If we reuse valuable resources,	**b.** if the wind blows.
_____ **8.** We will conserve gasoline	**c.** we will avoid accidents.
_____ **9.** If we are careful with nuclear power,	**d.** more people will have food.
_____ **10.** Wind-powered generators will produce energy	**e.** we will save energy.

Name _____ Date _____

GRAMMAR

Use after the lesson about future time.

Future Time

Future time is used to tell what will happen in the future. The simple future can be used to tell a future action or a future condition.

Future Action

The author of the letter will stay in his house on the same street.

Future Condition

When the new motor cars replace carriages, people will move around faster.

Rewrite each sentence below using *will* + a verb to tell a future action or condition.

Example: I hope we (live) here for another hundred years.

I hope we will live here for another hundred years.

1. One day the traffic (to be) so bad that we won't be able to cross the street.

   _____

2. Soon, we (have) a view that is nothing but buildings and pavement. _____

   _____

3. I don't think one-way streets (reduce) the number of accidents. _____

   _____

4. I am afraid that people (drive) even faster in the future. _____

   _____

5. Maybe people (realize) that they need to slow down.

   _____

   _____

SKILLS FOR WRITING

Use with textbook page 151.

Writing a Formal Persuasive Letter

The purpose of a **formal persuasive letter** is to persuade readers to change their beliefs, opinions, or behavior. When you write a formal letter, it is important to use the correct letter structure shown on page 151 of your student book.

The parts of the following persuasive letter are out of order. Read the letter. Then write the letter for each part on the line where it belongs. Two have been done for you.

a. The library closes at 6 P.M. every day of the week. I think it should stay open until 9 P.M. two nights this week. Shutting its doors at 6 P.M. means that students who have part-time jobs or play sports after school cannot get to the library before it closes. This makes it hard for us to study and to do research. Last week, fifty students signed a petition in favor of extending the library hours. I propose that the Town Council vote to keep the library open later two nights a week. I urge readers of this newspaper to call their council members about this situation! Thank you for your support!

b. Editor
Daily Times
Daily Times Ave.
Pine Grove, CA 89027

c. Sincerely,

d. March 23, 2003

e. 2019 Elm St.
Pine Grove, CA 89027

f. *Alex Gonzales*

g. Dear Editor:

1. _____

2. _____

3. _____

4. _____

5. _____

6. _____ c _____

7. _____ f _____

PROOFREADING AND EDITING

Use with textbook page 152.

Read the following letter carefully. Find the mistakes. Be sure to look for errors with *if* clauses and for mistakes in the organization of the letter. Rewrite the letter on the lines below. Make sure you correct all the mistakes!

May 19, 2003
24681 Rose Road
Emma Woods

The Town Daily
200 News Street
My Town, CA 00000

Yours truly,

    We need a traffic light at the corner of oak Street and Elm Avenue because it is the busiest intersection in town. Every week, there is at least one accident. Drivers don't stop. Last tuesday, someone who was using the crosswalk was nearly hit. If there is a light drivers slow down. Therefore, a light protects walkers, too. The state paid half the money if, the town pays the other half. We need a light now?

My Town, CA 00000
Dear Editor:

_____

_____

_____

_____

_____

_____

_____

_____

_____

_____

_____

_____

_____

_____

_____

SPELLING

Use after the spelling lesson.

Schwa

The **schwa sound** is a sound that a vowel letter *(a, e, i, o,* or *u)* can stand for in an unaccented syllable of a word. The schwa sound is pronounced *uh*. The vowel letter *i* in the unaccented syllable of *fossil* stands for the same sound—the schwa sound— that the vowel letter e stands for in the unaccented syllable of fu<u>e</u>l. Because each vowel letter can stand for the schwa sound, you may need to check a dictionary when you are spelling words with schwa sounds.

Read each word. Underline each unaccented syllable with a schwa sound. Then circle the vowel letter that stands for the schwa sound. Remember that some words have more than one unaccented syllable and schwa sound. Recall that some words may be spelled the same but have a different pronunciation and/or meaning. Use a dictionary if you need to.

Example: acc<u>ⓘd ⓔ</u>nt

1. affect

2. happen

3. produce

4. pollute

5. animal

6. common

7. focus

8. careful

9. consumer

10. typical

UNIT 4 Change
PART 2

Contents

VOCABULARY

Use with textbook page 155.

Read each sentence. Then circle the letter next to the word or words closest in meaning to the underlined word in the sentence. Follow the example.

Example: Mrs. Smith is the <u>principal</u> of our school, so she is in charge of everything.

(a.) head   b. student   c. driver   d. parent

1. We knew that it was a great <u>honor</u> to receive the medal for bravery.

a. disaster   b. disappointment   c. embarrassment   d. privilege

2. The delicious food was <u>proof</u> of her cooking ability.

a. joke   b. literature   c. evidence   d. article

3. The volunteer has a <u>reputation</u> in the community for her kind acts.

a. salary   b. trait someone is known for   c. trend   d. idea

4. The big <u>trend</u> this year is to wear white socks with black shoes.

a. fiction   b. style   c. freedom   d. problem

Read the clues. Use the words in the box to complete the crossword puzzle. (Hint: You will not use all of the words, and you will not use any word twice.)

proof	grade	worthy	disaster	principal
honor	trend	reputation	China	graduation

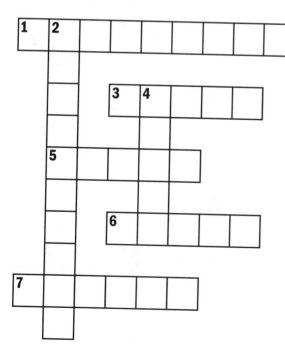

ACROSS

1. head of a school
3. a country in Asia
5. the latest movement or style
6. evidence that something is true
7. deserving; having value

DOWN

2. one's character, as it is judged by others
4. privilege

Name _____ Date _____

VOCABULARY BUILDING

Understanding Synonyms

Synonyms are words that mean the same or nearly the same. A word can have more than one synonym. To find synonyms, use a thesaurus, a dictionary, or a synonym finder on a computer. Read the synonyms on the following chart.

Word	Synonyms
big	large
little	small
difficult	hard
completed	finished
foreign	strange

Rewrite the sentences below. Replace the underlined word with a synonym from the chart.

1. Shirley's new classroom was <u>big</u>. _____

2. Shirley felt <u>little</u> compared to her classmates. _____

_____

3. *Mrs. Rappaport* was a <u>difficult</u> name for Shirley to pronounce. _____

_____

4. There was something <u>foreign</u> about the principal. _____

_____

5. Shirley had <u>completed</u> only three grades in China. _____

_____

Name _____ Date _____

READING STRATEGY

Use with textbook page 155.

Using Your Experience to Understand a Story

Using your own experience can help you understand a story. It can help you relate to what is happening in the story and understand how the characters feel and act. As you read, ask yourself these questions:

- Who is the main character? How am I like this character?
- What happens to the main character? Have I had similar experiences?
- What does the main character think or feel? Have I had similar thoughts or feelings?

Read pages 156 and 157 in your textbook. Then answer the questions.

1. What new experience does Shirley have?

_____

_____

2. Is the experience easy or difficult for her? Why?

_____

_____

3. How does Shirley feel about the new experience? Use words and examples from the story to explain how Shirley is feeling.

_____

_____

4. Have you or someone you know had a similar experience? How did you or that person feel?

_____

_____

5. How are you and Shirley alike? How are you different?

_____

_____

Use with textbook pages 164–166.

Summary: "Migration Patterns"

People in the United States move often. The selection provides facts about how many people move, where they move, and why they move. It also tells how the regions of the country are changing as a result of changes in their population.

Visual Summary

- People in the United States move often.
- Most move close to home.
- Young, single, or divorced people who earn less and own less property tend to move the most.
- The South has been the fastest-growing region.
- The Northeast has been losing the most people.

Use What You Know

List three things you know about moving.

1. _____

2. _____

3. _____

Text Structure: Informational Text

An informational text presents factual information to readers. Statistics are a type of fact that provides numbers or amounts. Underline a statistic in the first paragraph. What statement does the statistic support? Write it below.

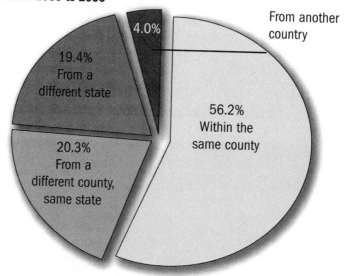

MARK THE TEXT

_____

_____

Reading Strategy: Using Graphs

When informational texts give statistics, they often make the statistic clearer by using graphs, special diagrams that show or compare amounts. A pie chart is a kind of graph that shows amounts as portions of a whole. Which statistics in the second paragraph does the pie chart on this page help you see and compare? Draw lines from the statistics in the paragraph to the four sections of the pie chart. What does the whole pie stand for?

MARK THE TEXT

_____

Migration Patterns

People in the United States move often. According to the United States Census Bureau, 43.3 million Americans—more than 15 percent of the total population—changed **residence** between March 1999 and March 2000.

In that year, the people who moved didn't always move a long distance. This pie chart shows that about 56 percent of them stayed within the same **county**. About 20 percent moved from a different county within the same state. About 20 percent moved from a different state. Only 4 percent moved from another country. Although the overall moving **rate** hasn't changed much in the past **decade**, people have tended to move longer distances since 1998. In 1998, almost 65 percent of people who moved stayed within the same county. Only 15 percent of those who moved went to another state.

Percent Distribution of Movers by Type of Move: March 1999 to 2000

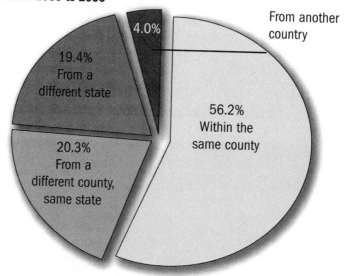

From another country

4.0%

19.4% From a different state

56.2% Within the same county

20.3% From a different county, same state

residence, where a person lives
county, part of a state
rate, the number of times something happens in a period of time
decade, ten years

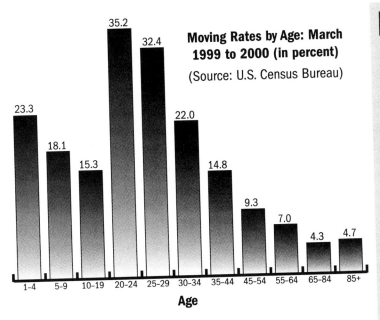

Moving Rates by Age: March 1999 to 2000 (in percent)
(Source: U.S. Census Bureau)

35.2 32.4
23.3 18.1 15.3 22.0 14.8 9.3 7.0 4.3 4.7

1-4 5-9 10-19 20-24 25-29 30-34 35-44 45-54 55-64 65-84 85+
Age

Moving rates vary according to such factors as age, marital status, property ownership, and income. The bar chart shows that in 1999–2000, about one-third of 25- to 29-year-olds moved, but less than 5 percent of peoples ages 65 to 84 moved. Younger people may have moved more often because they got married or because of new jobs. Single people and divorced people moved more often than married people. Widowed people moved least often, possibly because widowed people tend to be older. One-third of all renters moved in 1999–2000, compared with only 9 percent of homeowners. Finally, lower-income groups were more likely to move than higher-income groups.

---

marital status, being married or unmarried
income, money from your job; earnings
divorced people, people who have ended their marriage by law
widowed people, people whose husbands or wives have died

Comprehension Check

Underline the four factors that affect how often a person moves. Explain why and how you think owning property might affect someone's ability to move.

MARK THE TEXT

_____

_____

Reading Strategy: Using Graphs

A bar graph uses bars, or thick lines, to show and compare amounts. Labels on or near each bar explain what amount is being shown. On the bar graph on this page, circle the bar of the age group that moves the most. Also circle the label that tells what that age group is. By looking at the bar graph, what can you easily see about the amount older people move compared to others?

MARK THE TEXT

_____

_____

Comprehension Check

Underline the possible reason that younger people move more often than older people. Why do you think single or divorced people move more than married people?

MARK THE TEXT

_____

_____

_____

Unit 4 Change Part 2

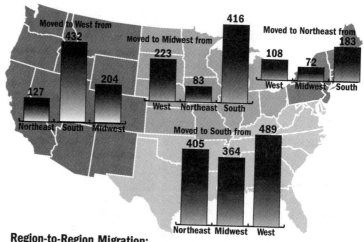

Region-to-Region Migration:
March 1999 to 2000 (in thousands)
(Source: U.S. Census Bureau)

Text Structure: Informational Text

Informational texts often give the meaning of key terms. Sometimes they do this in notes at the bottom of the page. Circle the note that defines the key term *population distribution*. What other terms are defined in the notes on this page? **MARK THE TEXT**

_____

_____

Reading Strategy: Using Graphic Aids

The titles of graphs often make the information on them clearer. In the title for the bar graphs on this page, underline the words that make the numbers on the graph clearer. According to the graphs, how many people moved from the West to the Northeast from March 1999 to 2000? **MARK THE TEXT**

_____

How many people moved from the Midwest to the South from March 1999 to 2000?

_____

Comprehension Check

Underline the information in the last paragraph that predicts what is likely to happen to the South in the future. Why do you think more Southerners may migrate to the West and Midwest? **MARK THE TEXT**

_____

  Moves to different regions in the United States have changed the country's **population distribution**. Look at the graphs above. As was true throughout the 1990s, more people moved from the Northeast to the South than from the South to the Northeast in 1999–2000. Many more people moved *from* the Northeast than *to* the Northeast. The number of people moving into and out of **urban** and **rural** areas remained about the same.

  What will the future population distribution of the United States look like? If today's trends continue, more people may be moving to the South. In addition, the new residents there may be younger than those moving to the South today. The Northeast may become less populated, and more Southerners may migrate to the **less densely populated** areas of the West and Midwest.

---

population distribution, pattern of where people live in an area
urban, relating to a town or city
rural, relating to the country, especially farmland
less densely populated, having fewer people

Retell It!

Choose one of the three graphic aids—the pie chart on page 164, the bar graph on page 165, or the map with bar graphs on page 166. Use your own words to retell the information that it contains.

_____

_____

_____

_____

_____

_____

_____

Reader's Response

What did you find most interesting about the information in this selection? Why?

_____

_____

_____

_____

_____

Think About the Skill

How did the graphs help you better understand the information in this selection?

_____

_____

_____

_____

GRAMMAR

Use with textbook page 168.

Complex Sentences

A complex sentence has an **independent clause** and a **dependent clause**.

An **independent clause** is a sentence. It has a subject and a verb and expresses a complete thought.

A **dependent clause** has a subject and verb, but it does not express a complete thought. A dependent clause usually begins with a **subordinating conjunction** such as *after, although, as, because, before, but, if, when,* or *while.*

An independent clause and a dependent clause together make a **complex sentence**. A comma is used when the dependent clause comes at the beginning of the sentence, before the independent clause.

Read each sentence below. Place a check mark (✔) in front of each complex sentence. Circle the subordinating conjunction.

_____ **1.** Shirley couldn't stop staring at the principal of her new school, P.S. 8.

_____ **2.** As Shirley continued to stare, her mother hissed at her to stop.

_____ **3.** When the schoolmistress winked at her, Shirley tried to wink back.

_____ **4.** It must be proper if a principal does it.

_____ **5.** Although Shirley tried hard to close just one eye, she shut both her eyes—twice!

_____ **6.** Shirley followed the schoolmistress to her new classroom.

_____ **7.** Shirley liked her teacher right away, although Mrs. Rappaport had a most difficult name.

_____ **8.** If she failed at school, Shirley knew she would be in trouble.

_____ **9.** When she looked around, Shirley hoped she would see a friendly face.

_____ **10.** Instead, she saw many friendly faces!

GRAMMAR

Use after the lesson about commas.

Using Commas

A **comma** is a punctuation mark used to separate words and phrases within a sentence.

Use commas:

- in a series or list: *We packed the boxes, loaded the truck, and drove away.*
- after introductory clauses: *After I was born, my family moved to the United States.*
- in a compound sentence: *My old home was nice, but I like my new home better.*
- in dialogue: *Dad said, "We need a bigger house."*
- in writing the greeting (*Dear Maria,*) and closing (*Sincerely, Ms. Fong*) of a letter
- in writing dates (*March 1, 1999*) and numbers (*10,000*)
- in writing names of cities and states (*Houston, Texas*)

Read each sentence. Add commas wherever they are missing and needed.

Example: People move from city to city[**,**] state to state[**,**] and country to country.

1. Because they have taken new jobs or gotten married many young people moved to a different state last year.

2. Although the overall moving rate hasn't changed much people have moved longer distances.

3. The survey was taken on March 15 1997.

4. A representative of the Census Bureau said "More than 15 percent of the total population moved."

5. One city that increased in population was Miami Florida.

Circle the commas that are in the wrong place. Draw an arrow to show where the comma or commas should be.

Example: Dear⌒Susan

6. Although, people often move to a new city to find work that is not the only reason.

7. Moving rates vary according to, age marital status and income.

8. The mayor, reported "We have people from fifty different nations living in our city."

9. The next city census will be taken on January, 15 2004.

10. After, the census is taken we will know exactly how many people live here.

SKILLS FOR WRITING

Use with textbook page 169.

Writing an Informal Persuasive E-mail Message

Persuasion is used in informal as well as in formal writing. Sometimes people write informal messages to try to persuade friends to do things. When you write an **informal persuasive** note or **E-mail message**, be sure to give reasons that support your position.

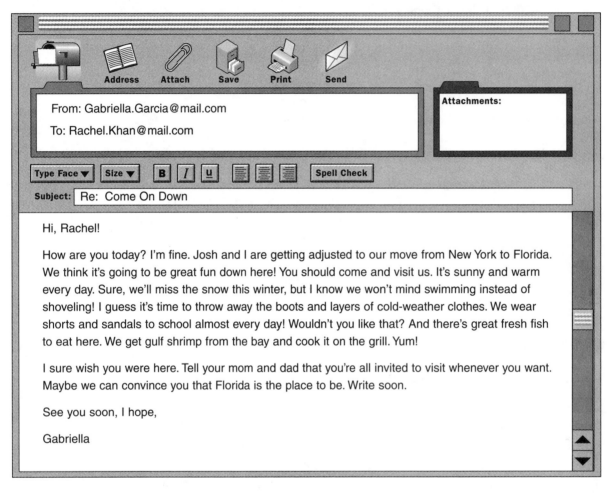

Address   Attach   Save   Print   Send

Attachments:

From: Gabriella.Garcia@mail.com

To: Rachel.Khan@mail.com

Type Face ▼   Size ▼   B   I   u   ▤ ▤ ▤   Spell Check

Subject: Re: Come On Down

Hi, Rachel!

How are you today? I'm fine. Josh and I are getting adjusted to our move from New York to Florida. We think it's going to be great fun down here! You should come and visit us. It's sunny and warm every day. Sure, we'll miss the snow this winter, but I know we won't mind swimming instead of shoveling! I guess it's time to throw away the boots and layers of cold-weather clothes. We wear shorts and sandals to school almost every day! Wouldn't you like that? And there's great fresh fish to eat here. We get gulf shrimp from the bay and cook it on the grill. Yum!

I sure wish you were here. Tell your mom and dad that you're all invited to visit whenever you want. Maybe we can convince you that Florida is the place to be. Write soon.

See you soon, I hope,

Gabriella

1. What is the purpose of the E-mail? _____

2. What is one thing Gabriella says to persuade Rachel about Florida?

_____

3. Give one example of informal language. _____

4. How is the end of the message different from the end of a formal letter?

_____

5. Why do you think Gabriella uses informal language in her E-mail?

_____

PROOFREADING AND EDITING

Use with textbook page 170.

Read the E-mail message carefully. Be sure to look for mistakes with complex sentences and use of commas. Rewrite the E-mail message on the lines below, beginning with the greeting. Correct all the mistakes!

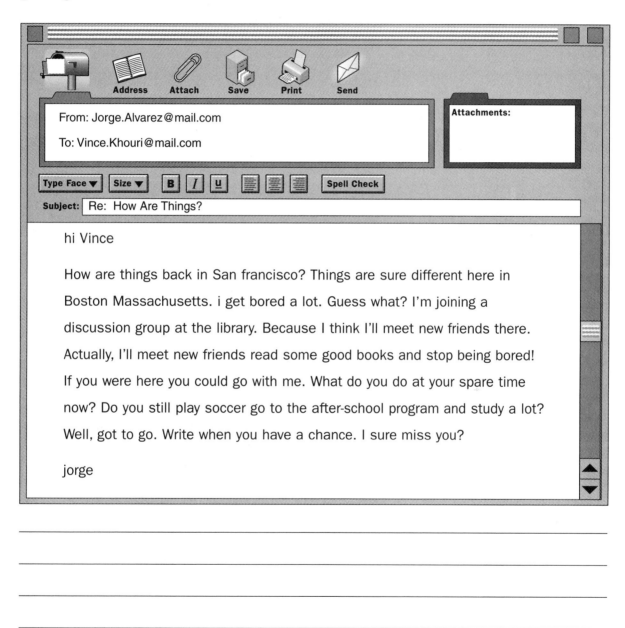

Address   Attach   Save   Print   Send

Attachments:

From: Jorge.Alvarez@mail.com

To: Vince.Khouri@mail.com

Type Face ▼   Size ▼   **B** *I* <u>U</u>   ☰ ☰ ☰   Spell Check

Subject: Re: How Are Things?

hi Vince

How are things back in San francisco? Things are sure different here in Boston Massachusetts. i get bored a lot. Guess what? I'm joining a discussion group at the library. Because I think I'll meet new friends there. Actually, I'll meet new friends read some good books and stop being bored! If you were here you could go with me. What do you do at your spare time now? Do you still play soccer go to the after-school program and study a lot? Well, got to go. Write when you have a chance. I sure miss you?

jorge

_____

_____

_____

_____

_____

_____

_____

_____

SPELLING

Use after the spelling lesson.

Rules for Plurals

A singular noun names one thing. A **plural** noun names more than one thing.

- To make most nouns plural, add -s: *years*, *rocks*, *records*, *rows*, *curls*.
- Add -es to nouns ending in *s, ss, ch, sh, z, x*: *dresses, wishes, boxes*.
- Add -es to nouns ending in a consonant + *o*: *heroes, tomatoes*.
- If a noun ends in a consonant + *y*, change the *y* to *i* and add -es: *stories, copies*.
- If a noun ends in *f* or *fe*, the *f* may change to a *v* before -es is added: *leaves, hooves*.
- Some nouns have irregular plurals: *children, geese, mice*.
- Some nouns do not change at all to form the plural: *sheep, species, fish*.

Read each sentence. Write the noun in parentheses ( ) in the plural form.

Example: She had been staring at the (stranger) *strangers* _____.

1. Shirley held up ten (finger) _____.

2. Mother only completed three (grade) _____.

3. All foreign (nose) _____ were higher than Chinese ones.

4. There were many new (rule) _____ to follow.

5. They brought their (lunch) _____ to school.

6. What were their (life)

   _____

   like after school?

7. Their (family) _____

   were from many different countries.

8. The (child) _____ stood

   up and waved at her.

9. Was there something wrong with her (eye)

   _____ ?

10. The (word)

    _____ sounded like

gurgling water.

UNIT 5 The Frontier

Contents

VOCABULARY

Use with textbook page 181.

Choose the word from the box that completes each sentence below. Use the context to help you. Write the word in the space provided. Use a dictionary if you need to.

| constitution | enforce | patriotism | political | siege |

1. The town held a Fourth of July parade to show its _____.

2. The soldiers protected the building from a _____ by the enemy.

3. When you register to vote, you can choose the _____ party that you want to join.

4. The job of the city's police is to _____ the city's laws.

5. The original copy of the state's _____ is preserved in a museum display case.

Read the clues. Use the words in the box to complete the crossword puzzle. (Hint: You will not use all of the words.)

| citizens | constitution | enforce | worship |
| politics | republic | southeastern | patriotism |

ACROSS

1. love for one's country
3. the written laws and principles of a nation or state that describe the government's powers and the people's rights
4. to make sure that people obey rules or laws

DOWN

2. a government ruled by the people
3. people who live in and belong to a country

VOCABULARY BUILDING

Understanding Antonyms

Antonyms are words that mean the opposite or almost the opposite of each other. Read the words and the antonyms in the chart.

Selection Word	Antonym
began	ended
independence	dependence
survive	perish
left	stayed
loyalty	disloyalty
tame	wild

Read the pairs of sentences below. Find the antonym pair in the chart that makes sense in each pair of sentences. Write the word that fits each sentence in the space provided.

Example: Life in the civilized area of the East was **tame**. Compared to life in the East, life in the frontier was **wild**.

1. Life on the frontier was hard, and some people did not _____.

   Many settlers saw their loved ones _____ from disease or other

   hardships.

2. The settlers felt _____ to America. The Mexican government

   thought their attitude showed _____ to Mexico and its laws.

3. More and more Texans wanted their _____ and freedom. They did

   not like their _____ on Mexico.

4. The Texans _____ their siege in October 1835. The siege finally

   _____ seven weeks later.

5. After Santa Anna took the Alamo, some frightened settlers _____

   Texas. However, many others _____ to fight at San Jacinto.

READING STRATEGY

Use with textbook pages 181.

Taking Notes

Taking notes will help you remember information when you read. When you read a social studies text, your notes can help you review events in **chronological order**, the order in which the events happened.

Read the first section of "The Road to Texas Independence" on pages 182–183 in your textbook. As you read, complete the chart below. Take notes in the right column about the events that occurred on the dates listed in the left column.

	Dates in Chronological Order	Events
1.	Early 1800s	
2.	1821	
3.	1823	
4.	1829	
5.	1833	

Use with textbook pages 190–192.

Summary: from *A Line in the Sand*

This selection presents fictional entries from a thirteen-year-old girl's journal. Lucinda tells how she and her family feel about living in Texas in 1835. Lucinda's brother and uncle want to fight Mexico to make Texas independent, but Lucinda's father hates war and thinks the Mexican army is too big to fight. Lucinda does not think war will come but worries that her family will have to leave Texas if there is a war.

Visual Summary

Entry Date	Main Points
early on Wednesday, September 16, 1835	Letter arrives from Uncle Henry in War Party, which favors fighting for Texas independence. Lucinda's father is in the Peace Party, which wants to avoid war and work under Mexican rule for a democratic constitution.
later on Wednesday, September 16, 1835	Lucinda's father and brother Willis argue about Texas independence over dinner. Willis sees a fight for freedom, but Papa has fought in earlier wars and thinks fighting Mexico would be too costly.
Thursday, September 17, 1835	Lucinda says that she doesn't really believe war will come. She hopes she will never have to leave Texas, which she loves.

from *A Line in the Sand*

Sherry Garland

Use What You Know

List three things you know about Texas.

1. _____

2. _____

3. _____

Literary Element: Setting

The setting is the time and place of a work. Underline details that tell the day and place where this work is set. During what historical period is it set?

🖉 **MARK THE TEXT**

_____

_____

Text Structure: Historical Fiction

Historical fiction combines real facts about the past with invented characters, such as Lucinda and her family, and situations. Underline the factual information about the two rival political parties in Texas in 1835.

🖉 **MARK THE TEXT**

Reading Strategy: Identifying with a Character

Identifying with a character can help you understand and enjoy a text. Consider what you have in common with the character. Circle a thought or feeling that Lucinda reveals on this page. Did you identify with her feelings? If so, explain how.

🖉 **MARK THE TEXT**

_____

Wednesday, September 16

A man from San Felipe, in Austin's Colony, rode through town today. San Felipe is over a hundred miles northeast of here, on the Brazos River, and is the hub of the Texas colonies. It even has a printing press. The rider dropped off letters and a stack of the *Telegraph and Texas Register* newspaper. How I love reading those wrinkled, inky-smelling pages.

We received a letter from Mama's brother, Henry, who lives with his wife, Nancy, and five children in San Felipe. Uncle Henry has decided to move to DeWitt's Colony next spring. When Papa heard the news, he didn't say a word. He just walked out onto the gallery and washed his face. Papa's never admitted it out loud, but I don't think he likes Uncle Henry much. Uncle Henry belongs to the War Party—he wants Texas to declare her independence from Mexico. Papa belongs to the Peace Party—he wants Texas to stay part of Mexico and urge a democratic constitution. Papa hates war. He says he saw enough killing in the War of 1812, serving under Andrew Jackson, who is now president of the United States.

_____

hub, center
gallery, porch
party, group of people with the same opinions about government
urge, suggest strongly
democratic, governed by the citizens themselves

Later That Day—

After supper Papa looked up from the newspaper and said, "It's just a handful of slick lawyers and fool agitators causing all this talk about war. Most of the colonists are farmers like me who want to live out their lives and raise their families and not get involved in politics."

Says Willis, "I've heard there are thirty thousand Americans settled in Texas now, and only four thousand Mexicans. If this were a democracy, the majority would rule. But this isn't America, it's Mexico, and Texians have no say in government affairs. That ain't right." Willis is just seventeen, but he talks like he knows everything.

Says Papa, "The Mexican army is one of the biggest in the world. Even if the Texians fought a war and won, it would be a costly victory."

Willis jumped up from the table and said, "But Papa, we can't just stand by and give up our freedoms. Grandpa Lawrence fought in the American Revolution, didn't he? And you fought the British at Horseshoe Bend. When it comes my turn to fight for freedom, I'll not turn my back."

Papa shook his head as Willis left the room. Mama looked up from poking the fire logs and said, "Now, don't those words sound mighty familiar,

_____

handful of slick lawyers, small number of persuasive
   lawyers who are smart but not to be trusted
fool agitators, silly political troublemakers
majority, more than half of any total
turn my back, refuse to help

Literary Element: Setting

Setting can refer to specific times and places as well as more general ones. Circle the time of day that the events on this page take place. Where in the Lawrence home do they take place?

MARK THE TEXT

_____

Text Structure: Historical Fiction

The events in 1830s Texas history continue to affect the characters in this section. Underline one reason Papa gives for avoiding war. What is Willis's opinion on the issue, and what are his reasons?

MARK THE TEXT

_____

_____

_____

Comprehension Check

Circle the information Mama mentions about Papa's past. Why do you think she brings this memory up at this time? Underline Lucinda's attitude toward the war.

_____

_____

_____

Literay Element: Setting

Underline three details that Lucinda gives about the area where she lives. What is her attitude about this part of Texas?

_____

_____

Reading Strategy: Identifying with a Character

Circle a sentence where Lucinda expresses her feelings. Do they help you identify with her character? Why or why not?

_____

_____

_____

_____

Mr. Lawrence? I recollect you getting all fired up twenty-nigh years ago and running off to join the Georgia volunteers."

Papa snorted, then got quiet, lost in his memories.

Thursday, September 17

Talk of war has been going on all summer. Sometimes it scares me, but I think it is just talk. I don't believe war will really come. We are American born, but now we are Mexican citizens, for Texas is part of the Republic of Mexico. We came for the fertile, cheap land and the chance to farm and make a decent living.

Those early times were hard; some gave up, but not Papa. He says our roots are sunk too deep into Texas soil to pull up now. I think the worst is behind us and only good looms on the horizon. Our cotton crop is the grandest we've ever had, the town is growing, and a schoolhouse is to be built next spring. And the land is so unspoiled and beautiful—sometimes my heart fills up with so much joy and freedom, I have to whoop and run across the prairie like a wild mustang. I pray we never, never leave this place.

_____

recollect, remember
all fired up, very excited
twenty-nigh, almost twenty
snorted, noisily forced air out through the nose, to express anger
fertile, good for farming
decent, good enough
pull up, move away
looms on the horizon, will happen in the future
whoop, shout
prairie, large area of land in North America covered with grass
mustang, small wild horse

Retell It!

This work of historical fiction is told in a series of imaginary journal entries written by Lucinda. Retell one of those entries from the viewpoint of a different character.

_____

_____

_____

_____

_____

_____

_____

Reader's Response

If you had been a member of Lucinda's family, would you have supported the War Party or the Peace Party? Why?

_____

_____

_____

_____

Think About the Skill

How did identifying with Lucinda's character help you better understand the selection? Was there any other character you identified with? If so, who was this person, and why did you identify with him or her?

_____

_____

_____

_____

GRAMMAR

Use with textbook page 194.

Comparative and Superlative Adjectives
Read the following rules for forming **comparative adjectives.**

- Use the **comparative** form of adjectives and the word *than* to compare two things:
  a. Add *-er* to most one-syllable adjectives and some two-syllable adjectives:
  small—small*er than*   pretty—prett*ier than*.
  b. Use *more* before most adjectives that have two or more syllables:
  enthusiastic—*more* enthusiastic *than*.

- Use the **superlative** form of adjectives and the word *the* to compare three or more things:
  c. Add *-est* to one-syllable adjectives: small—*the* smallest.
  d. Use *the most* before adjectives of two or more syllables: eager—*the most* eager.

- Some adjectives have irregular comparative and superlative forms:
  e.

Adjective	Comparative form	Superlative form
good	*better than*	*the best*
bad	*worse than*	*the worst*

Read each sentence below. Circle the comparative or superlative adjective in each sentence. Then decide which rule at the top of the page describes this adjective form. Write the rule's letter (**a** through **e**) in the space provided.

_____ **1.** By the 1830s, the number of American settlers in Texas was larger than the Mexican population in Texas.

_____ **2.** The first settlers faced more difficult problems than later settlers faced.

_____ **3.** San Felipe was one of the most important towns in the Texas colonies.

_____ **4.** For Lucinda, the best piece of mail was the newspaper.

_____ **5.** Politics was not the greatest concern of many Texans.

_____ **6.** Papa thought that peace was more important than war.

_____ **7.** Uncle Henry thought war would be better than living under the Mexican laws.

_____ **8.** The Mexican army was one of the largest in the world.

_____ **9.** The number of Texans in favor of war was smaller than the number in favor of peace.

_____ **10.** To Lucinda, Texas was the most beautiful place in the world.

GRAMMAR

Use after the lesson about comparative and superlative adverbs.

Comparative and Superlative Adverbs

The rules for using **adverbs that compare** are similar to the rules for using adjectives that compare. Adverbs usually describe verbs. Sometimes they describe adjectives.

- Use the **comparative** form of adverbs and the word *than* to compare two items:
  a. Add *-er* to most one-syllable adverbs: *ran fast—ran faster than*.
  b. Use *more* before adverbs of two or more syllables: *packed densely—packed more densely*.

- Use the **superlative** form of adverbs and *the* to compare three or more things:
  c. Add *-est* to one-syllable adverbs: *played hard—played the hardest*.
  d. Use *the most* before adverbs of two or more syllables: *spoke clearly—spoke the most* clearly.

- Some adverbs have irregular comparative and superlative forms:
  e.

Adverb	Comparative form	Superlative form
well	better than	the best
badly	worse than	the worst

Read each sentence below. Circle the comparative or superlative adverb in each sentence. Match it with the correct rule above, *a* through *e*. Write the correct letter in the space provided.

_____ **1.** In the 1800s, the eastern part of the country was more densely populated than the frontier.

_____ **2.** For a few years, Texas grew the fastest of all the territories.

_____ **3.** The settlers worked more eagerly than they ever had before.

_____ **4.** People could obtain land more easily in Texas than in other places.

_____ **5.** Moses Austin tried harder than anybody else to start a colony in Texas.

_____ **6.** Stephen Austin talked better than the other Texans and convinced more people to come to Texas.

_____ **7.** The constitution was the most clearly written document that Texans had ever produced.

_____ **8.** The settlers felt more closely connected to the United States than to Mexico.

_____ **9.** Santa Anna fought the hardest of all the soldiers at San Jacinto.

_____ **10.** Of all Santa Anna's actions, the American colonists and Tejanos reacted most strongly to his decision to make himself Mexico's dictator.

SKILLS FOR WRITING

Use with textbook page 195.

Taking Notes for a Research Report

Reread "Taking Notes for a Research Report" on page 195 in your textbook. Now imagine you are doing research on Sam Houston for your report. Begin by reading the following sample paragraph you might find in a resource book about Texas leaders.

> Both Sam Houston and Stephen Austin were born in Virginia in 1793. Houston grew up in Tennessee, and Austin grew up in Missouri. Both men served in the United States military. Houston was elected governor of Tennessee in 1827 but later resigned. He moved to Texas in 1832. Austin approved Houston's request for a land permit. Houston opened a law practice. In 1835 Houston was appointed major general of the Texas army. Austin and Houston agreed that Texas should become independent from Mexico. Houston guided the army during the war with Mexico. Both men wanted to be the first president of the Republic of Texas, but Houston won the election. Austin served as secretary of state until his death in December 1836. Houston later became governor of the state of Texas.

Remember, the topic of your report is Sam Houston. Therefore, you should focus on information about Houston, not Stephen Austin.

Here is an example of a note card you might write. Always write a heading for your note card so that you can organize your cards before you write your paper. Notice that the wording on the card is brief. Fill in the card with information from the above paragraph.

Houston's Early Life and His Activities in Texas

He was born in the year _____ in the state of _____.
             1.   **2.**

He grew up in _____.
                  3.

Before moving to Texas, he _____ but _____.
                        4.   **5.**

When he came to Texas in _____, he _____.
                6.   **7.**

During the war for Texas independence, Houston _____.
                                            8.

After the war, he won _____.
                            9.

Later, Houston became _____.
                            10.

PROOFING AND EDITING

Use with textbook page 196.

Read the paragraph below carefully. Find the mistakes. Proofread carefully for mistakes in capitalization, punctuation, and comparative and superlative adjectives. If necessary, use a dictionary to check spelling. Rewrite the paragraph correctly on the lines below.

Houston and austin are two cities that has similarities and differences. One similarity is that they both are in texas. Houston is far south than Austin. They are both old cities, named after famus Texas pioneers, but Austin is slightly oldest than Houston. Huston is bigger than Austin, but Austin is the capital city of the State. houston is closer to the ocean. If you like the beach, its not far to Galveston bay from Houston. Some people thank the restaurents in Austin are best than the ones in Houston Some think that Houston has worst traffic than Austin. Do you want to no what I think. I think they are both great cities. Go to both citys and compare them for yourself! You can enjoy the sights the foods, and the fun of both.

_____

_____

_____

_____

_____

_____

_____

_____

_____

_____

_____

_____

SPELLING

Use after the spelling lesson.

Changing *y* to *i* to Add *-er* and *-est*

When you use comparative and superlative adjectives that end in *y*, follow this special spelling rule: When the letter before the *y* is a consonant, change the *y* to *i* before you add *-er* or *-est*. For example, in the adjective *rocky*, the letter *k* is a consonant. Change the *y* to *i* before you add *-er*, as in *rockier*, or *-est*, as in *rockiest*.

Complete the chart below by writing the comparative and superlative forms of each adjective. The first one has been done for you.

Adjective	Comparative	Superlative
busy	*busier*	*busiest*
scary	1.	2.
early	3.	4.
bumpy	5.	6.
shiny	7.	8.
lucky	9.	10.
heavy	11.	12.
funny	13.	14.
pretty	15.	16.

Write a sentence using the comparative or superlative form of the adjective in parentheses.

17. (angry) _____

_____

18. (mighty) _____

_____

19. (sleepy) _____

_____

20. (tiny) _____

_____

UNIT 5 The Frontier

PART 2

Contents

VOCABULARY

Use with textbook page 199.

Use a word from the box to complete each sentence.

| affection | cowboy | curious | pack | promise |

1. The _____ tied his horse, Rusty, to a tree trunk.

2. He patted Rusty's head with _____.

3. "I _____ that I won't be gone long," said the cowboy.

4. "I'm just _____ to know what's inside that cave!"

5. But he stopped outside the cave when he heard the _____ of wolves howl.

Read the clues. Use the words in the box to complete the crossword puzzle. (Hint: You will not use all the words.)

| promise | dug | curious | western | cowboy |
| rivers | covered | introduce | den | affection |

ACROSS

1. great liking for someone or something
5. to pledge to do or provide

DOWN

2. eager to know or find out; inquisitive
3. someone who herds and takes care of cattle
4. home of such wild animals as bears, foxes, and coyotes

Unit 5 The Frontier Part 2

VOCABULARY BUILDING

Understanding Resources for Meaning and Spelling

You can find information about words in a dictionary, a thesaurus, or on a computer. In a dictionary, bold **guidewords** at the top of each page tell you the first and last words listed alphabetically on that page. A word entry in a dictionary lists that word's **spelling**, **pronunciation**, **part of speech**, **meaning**, and **other forms**. Some dictionaries also include a **word history**. Below is an example of the guidewords and one entry word that appear on a dictionary page.

frog ● frugal

fron·tier (frən-**tir** *or* **frən**-tir) *noun* **1.** A region that forms the margin of settled territory. **2.** The border between two countries. **3.** A subject or an area of research that is just beginning to be understood, as in *the frontier of medicine*. [ME *fronter*, MF frontiere, OF *front*]

Use the above examples to answer the questions. Write your answer in the space provided.

1. What are the guidewords for the page that includes *frontier*?

    _____   _____

2. What is the first pronunciation for *frontier*? _____

3. What part of speech is *frontier*? _____

4. Which meaning defines *frontier* as it is used in Unit 5? _____

5. How many words are included in the word history of *frontier*? _____

READING STRATEGY

Use with textbook page 199.

Summarizing

Summarizing means restating the main ideas of a text in shorter form. Summarizing helps you find and recall the most important ideas.

First, read the steps for summarizing on page 199 in your textbook. Then read the beginning of the excerpt from *Pecos Bill: The Greatest Cowboy of All Time* on pages 201 and 202 in your textbook. Next, complete the chart by writing answers to each question. Use your own words.

Main Ideas

1. How did the family find out that Pecos Bill was missing?

   _____

   _____

2. What did his family do about it?

   _____

   _____

3. How did the boy and Grandy meet?

   _____

   _____

4. Where did Grandy take the boy?

   _____

   _____

5. What did Grandy teach Cropear?

   _____

   _____

Use with textbook pages 208–210.

Summary: "The Cowboy Era"

This passage tells about a time when many cowboys worked in Texas. Cowboys helped move cattle north to places where the animals were sold for high prices. These trips were long and hard. The cowboys wore special clothes to do their jobs. They did not get paid much money or get much sleep. After fences were built and railroads came to Texas, the cattle drives stopped, and the time of the cowboy ended.

Visual Summary

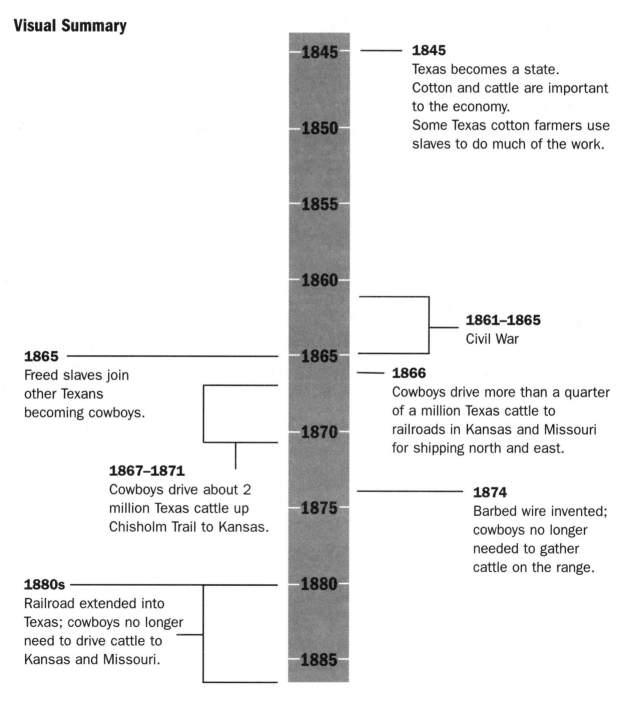

1845
Texas becomes a state.
Cotton and cattle are important to the economy.
Some Texas cotton farmers use slaves to do much of the work.

1861–1865
Civil War

1866
Cowboys drive more than a quarter of a million Texas cattle to railroads in Kansas and Missouri for shipping north and east.

1874
Barbed wire invented; cowboys no longer needed to gather cattle on the range.

1865
Freed slaves join other Texans becoming cowboys.

1867–1871
Cowboys drive about 2 million Texas cattle up Chisholm Trail to Kansas.

1880s
Railroad extended into Texas; cowboys no longer need to drive cattle to Kansas and Missouri.

The Cowboy Era

Use What You Know

List three things you know about cowboys.

1. _____

2. _____

3. _____

Text Structure:
Social Studies Article

Social studies articles often give information about historical events and their dates. Circle the first year mentioned in this article and the event that took place then. What war did the cowboy era follow? What were the dates of that war?

_____

_____

MARK THE TEXT

Reading Strategy: Summarizing

When you summarize, you restate the main idea and key details. Underline the part of the question in the second paragraph that you think expresses the main idea of the paragraph. What other details seem important enough to include in a summary of that paragraph?

_____

_____

_____

_____

MARK THE TEXT

Cotton and Cattle

Both cotton and cattle were important to the Texas economy when Texas became a state in 1845. Growing cotton was a lot of work. Most farmers planted, harvested, and picked their own cotton. Others were slaveholders, and enslaved Africans did much of the work. After the Civil War (1861–1865), the slaves were free. Many former slaves became sharecroppers. Others joined the growing number of Texans who became cowboys. They herded cattle on the large, open grasslands, called ranges.

Why were cattle important to the Texas economy? Beef was a popular food among Americans. In 1865, people in the northern and eastern United States didn't raise many cattle. Cattle there cost up to forty dollars a head. However, there were more than 4 million longhorn cattle in southern Texas. Cattle in Texas were worth only about four dollars a head. Ranchers quickly realized that they could make a lot of money by selling their cattle elsewhere. First, they could drive the cattle to Kansas or Missouri. There they could ship them to the northern or eastern United States by train. This idea led to the first cattle drives.

---

cattle, cows raised on a ranch
economy, a state's or nation's business and money system
sharecroppers, people who farm land that other people own; sharecroppers get part of the crop as pay
herded, made animals move together as a group by humans on horseback and by their dogs
a head, each animal
ranchers, people who own or work on large cattle farms
drives, acts of herding large groups of animals to another place

The Great Cattle Drives

In 1866, the great cattle drives began. In that year, cowboys drove more than a quarter of a million Texas cattle through what is now Oklahoma to Kansas and Missouri. This was a journey of about 1,609 to 2,414 kilometers (1,000 to 1,500 miles), and it took from three to six months to complete. The cowboys and cattle usually traveled on trails that already existed. About 2 million cattle were driven up the Chisholm Trail to Kansas between 1867 and 1871.

Cowboy Life

Cowboys did not have an easy job. Cattle drives were difficult and sometimes dangerous. Cowboys got little pay, worked long days, and got little sleep. River crossings and stampedes were particularly dangerous. Cowboys and cattle might drown crossing a river or get trampled to death in a stampede. Cowboys sometimes had to fight rustlers who tried to steal their cattle.

Some days were scorching hot, and some nights were freezing cold. Cowboys wore practical clothes to help them withstand these temperatures.

Cowboy hats had to be strong and long lasting. On hot days, the high top part of the hat kept the head cool, while the broad brim shaded the eyes and neck. On rainy or snowy days, the hats worked as umbrellas. The hats also protected cowboys from thorns and low-hanging branches. Cowboys used them to carry water, to fan or put out fires, and as pillows.

----

stampedes, sudden movements of large groups of running
  animals
practical, useful and sensible

**Text Structure:
Social Studies Article**

Social studies includes not only history but geography, or the layout of the land. Underline the distance of some of the great cattle drives and the states where the drives ended. Why were the cattle driven to those states?

_____

_____

Comprehension Check

Underline where the cowboys and cattle usually traveled, according to the first paragraph. From where to where did they go on the Chisholm Trail?

_____

_____

Reading Strategy: Summarizing

Headings can give you clues of the main ideas to summarize. Circle the two headings on this page. What main points does the article make about the subject in each heading?

_____

_____

_____

_____

_____

Comprehension Check

For what did cowboys use their scarves or bandannas?

_____

_____

Reading Strategy: Summarizing

Underline four words in the first paragraph on this page that sum up the main idea of the last two paragraphs of page 133. Besides the main idea, what details about a cowboy's life would you include in a summary of these paragraphs?

MARK THE TEXT

_____

_____

_____

Text Structure: Social Studies Article

Social studies articles often explore the causes or effects of historical events. Circle two developments or changes that caused the cowboy era to end. Why did these help end the era?

MARK THE TEXT

_____

_____

_____

The cowboys' other clothing was also practical. Their shirts and pants were made of strong material. They lasted a long time and protected the cowboys' skin. When it was dusty, cowboys covered their noses and mouths with the bandannas they wore around their necks.

When riding horses, they could rest the high heels of their boots in the stirrups. When roping cattle, they could dig the heels into the ground.

Many cowboys were native Texans. Others came from the South, East, and Midwest. Some were African American, Native American, and Mexican. They all had excellent riding skills, enabling them to herd cattle on long drives.

End of the Cowboy Era

The cowboy era lasted only about twenty years. During that time, thousands of cowboys worked on cattle drives. What caused the end of the cowboy era? Until the 1870s, the ranges were open; there were no fences to stop the movement of cattle. However, in 1874, barbed wire was invented. Farmers and ranchers began fencing their land with barbed wire, so the ranges became closed. In addition, many railroads were built in Texas in the 1880s. Then ranchers could send their cattle to market directly by train, so cattle drives became unnecessary.

---

protected, kept safe from damage
stirrups, metal rings where you put your feet when you ride a horse
roping, catching an animal with a circle of rope (lasso)
barbed wire, wire with short, sharp points on it
fencing, building wood or wire structures to stop people or animals from entering or leaving an area
unnecessary, not needed

Retell It!

Retell a section of the article as a song that a cowboy might have sung or a diary entry the cowboy might have written. Include the cowboy's activities, goals, thoughts, and feelings.

_____

_____

_____

_____

_____

_____

_____

Reader's Response

What new insights or ideas about the cowboy era did you get from reading this article?

_____

_____

_____

_____

Think About the Skill

How did summarizing help you absorb the information in this article?

_____

_____

_____

_____

GRAMMAR

Use with textbook page 212.

Using Possessive Adjectives and Possessive Pronouns
A **possessive pronoun** takes the place of a **possessive adjective + a noun**.

Complete the sentence in the column on the right. Use the possessive pronoun that means the same as the possessive adjective + a noun in the left column. Follow the example.

Possessive Adjective + Noun	Possessive Pronoun
That poodle is not **my dog**.	That poodle is not **mine**.
Is this **your paper**?	**1.** Is this _____?
The gray mare is **his horse**.	**2.** The gray mare is _____.
Her horse has gray spots.	**3.** _____ has gray spots.
Our ranch is in the hills.	**4.** _____ is in the hills.
The man bought **their cattle**.	**5.** The man bought _____.

In each pair of sentences below, circle the possessive adjective + noun in the first sentence. Underline the possessive pronoun in the second sentence.

6. Look at our store! Ours is the one with the blue door.

7. Their bags are at the register. Theirs are the green ones.

8. Is this bandanna part of your purchase? Are these shirts yours, too?

9. Please get my boots. The brown ones are mine.

10. The clerk will put her shirt in a bag. The red one is hers.

GRAMMAR

Use after the lesson about subject and object pronouns.

Subject and Object Pronouns
A **subject pronoun** replaces a noun that is the subject of a sentence.

> Sally Ann Thunder Ann Whirlwind Crockett is a tall-tale character. (noun)
> She has a really long name! (subject pronoun)

An **object pronoun** replaces a noun that is the object of a sentence. A noun or pronoun in the object position tells who or what receives the action expressed by the verb. The object noun or pronoun usually follows the verb.

> Sally Ann Thunder Ann married Davy Crockett. (noun after the verb)
> Sally Ann Thunder Ann married him. (object pronoun)

Read the sentences below. Circle the pronoun in parentheses ( ) that can replace the underlined noun.

1. Sally Ann was born in Kentucky. (She/Her)

2. Her large family welcomed Sally Ann. (she/her)

3. Even as a baby, Sally Ann could outrun her brothers. (them/they)

4. Sally Ann could swim like a fish and run like a cheetah. (He/She)

5. When she got older, she met Davy Crockett in the forest. (him/he)

6. Davy Crockett needed help. (He/Him)

Complete each sentence with a word from the box. Capitalize words as needed.
(Hint: You will not use all the words.)

he	we	him	she	I	they	it	her	you

_____ am reading another tall tale about Mike Fink.
      7.

_____ was known as King of the Keelboat Men. The Keelboat Men knew
      8.

that Mike was a great wrestler. One day, Mike met Sally Ann and wrestled with

_____ Sally Ann threw him clear into the next state! I think
      9.

_____ would like this tale.
      10.

SKILLS FOR WRITING

Use with textbook page 213.

Writing Summaries and Responses

A **summary** gives the main ideas of a text in short form. A summary does not include your personal reaction to a text. A **response** includes your thoughts and feelings about a text.

On workbook page 130, you summarized the beginning of the excerpt from *Pecos Bill: The Greatest Cowboy of All Time* by answering main-idea questions. Read the end of the excerpt on pages 204–205 in your textbook. Complete your summary by answering the questions below.

1. Who did Grandy introduce Cropear to?

_____

_____

2. Why did Grandy want to introduce Cropear to them?

_____

_____

3. How did the animals react to Grandy's request?

_____

_____

4. Why did the Wouser get angry with Grandy?

_____

_____

5. What happens to Cropear? Why?

_____

_____

6-10. Now write a five-sentence response to the selection in the space provided below. Remember that your response should include your personal reaction to the text.

_____

_____

_____

_____

_____

PROOFREADING AND EDITING

Use with textbook page 214.

Read the following response to a tall tale carefully. Find the mistakes. Be sure that all the possessive adjectives and possessive pronouns are used correctly. Rewrite the response correctly on the lines below.

My Response to "Pecos Bill Meets Slue-Foot Sue"

Me mom always says, "There's a lid for every pot." That means that everyone has a perfect friend somewhere in the world. When I read "Pecos Bill Meets Slue-Foot Sue," I thot about her words.

When Bill first saw Sue, he couldn't believe Bill's eyes! She was feistyer and toughest than any other woman he had known. Sue was much like bill. I liked it when them became good friends.

one part of the story that I didnt like was where the other cow boys were talking to Sue. I liked it better when just Bill and Sue was talking because they words were so funny. I liked getting to know two of the funnyest and stronger characters I've ever read about.

_____

_____

_____

_____

_____

_____

_____

_____

_____

_____

SPELLING

Use after the spelling lesson.

Spelling *kn-* Words

In some words, the sound that the letter *n* stands for is spelled *kn*. The *k* is silent. You can check a dictionary to see how words are spelled.

Read the words in the box. Write the words in which the *k* is silent.

knew	keep	kind	know	knob
knot	kilometers	knight	Kansas	

1. _____   4. _____

2. _____   5. _____

3. _____

Use a dictionary to find five more words that begin with *kn-*. List each word. Then write a sentence using each word.

6. _____

_____

_____

7. _____

_____

_____

8. _____

_____

_____

9. _____

_____

_____

10. _____

_____

_____

UNIT 6 Observing the Universe

PART 1

Contents

VOCABULARY

Use with textbook page 225.

Complete each sentence. Use words from the box. You will use each word once. Look at the diagram of Earth on page 225 of your textbook for help.

Northern Hemisphere   equator   rotation   North Pole   axis

1. The spinning motion of Earth is called its _____.

2. Canada and the United States are both in the _____.

3. Earth rotates around an imaginary line called its _____.

4. The farthest point north on Earth is the _____.

5. The imaginary line around the center of Earth is the _____.

Read the clues. Use words from the box to complete the crossword puzzle. (Hint: You will not use all the words.)

Northern Hemisphere   faces   orbit   tilted   South Pole
Southern Hemisphere   axis   direct   moon   North Pole

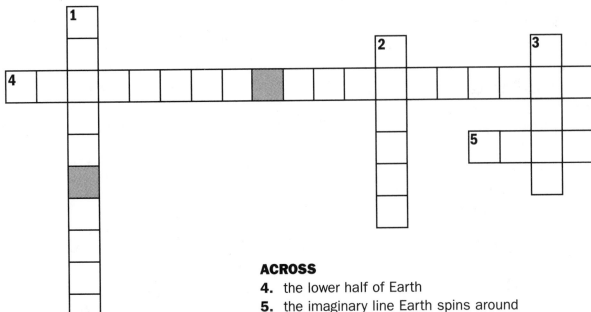

ACROSS
4. the lower half of Earth
5. the imaginary line Earth spins around
DOWN
1. the southernmost point on Earth
2. at an angle; not upright
3. the path in space that a planet or moon follows

VOCABULARY BUILDING

Understanding Homographs

Homographs are words that are spelled alike, but have different meanings, or origins, or pronunciations. You can figure out which meaning of a word is being used by the word's context in a sentence.

Read the sentences below. The underlined words are homographs. Find the meaning that the homograph has in the sentence. Circle the letter for the correct meaning.

1. It's peaceful to angle in a quiet lake.

   a. a sloping line   **b.** to fish with a hook and line

2. It's very cold at the North Pole.

   a. end of Earth's axis   **b.** a long piece of wood or other material

3. The Egyptian calendar had five days left at the end of the year.

   a. remaining   **b.** direction opposite of right

4. Sunlight can't reach the side of the Earth that faces away from the sun, so it is dark (night) there.

   a. to support someone   **b.** part of a surface of something
   in an argument

5. They like fall, so they moved North.

   a. a season of the year   **b.** to drop

6. They used moon cycles as a kind of calendar.

   a. a type   **b.** thoughtful

7. As Earth rotates to the east, the sun appears to set in the west.

   a. a collection   **b.** go down

8. The area around the equator receives a lot of direct sunlight.

   a. to order or command   **b.** without anything coming between

9. In the summer I long for the cool days of winter.

   a. wish or want   **b.** a measure greater than average

10. I read a story about the origin of the seasons.

   a. a telling or account of an event   **b.** a floor of a building

READING STRATEGY

Use with textbook page 225.

Studying Diagrams

A **diagram** is a drawing or plan that explains something. Science texts often have diagrams with labels.

When you read a science text with diagrams, remember to do the following:

- Read the section of the text.
- See if there is a diagram that goes with it.
- Study the diagram.
- Read any labels and captions on the diagram.
- Reread the text.

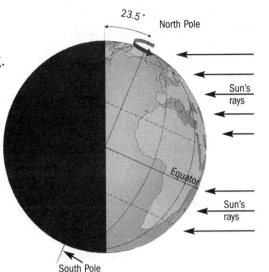

Read the text on page 226 in your textbook. Study the diagram. Then answer the following questions.

1. What does the diagram show? _____

2. What does the Earth rotate around? _____

3. What information about the Earth's rotation is in the diagram's caption but not the

   text on page 226? _____

Now, skim the text and focus on the diagrams on pages 228 and 229 in your textbook. Answer the following questions.

4. Where are the tropics? _____

5. Where does the Earth get the most direct sunlight? _____

   _____

6. Where does the Earth get less direct sunlight? _____

7. Why are temperatures coldest at the poles? _____

   _____

8. Where are temperatures warmest? Why? _____

   _____

9. Where are there four seasons? _____

   _____

10. What do you think the curved arrow at the North Pole is meant to show you?

   _____

Use with textbook pages 234–236.

Summary:

"How Glooskap Found the Summer" and
"Persephone and the Pomegranate Seeds"

People long ago told these stories to explain why Earth has different seasons. The Native American myth about Glooskap explains why Summer and Winter take turns ruling Glooskap's country. The Greek myth tells of Persephone, the daughter of the goddess of agriculture. It explains why Persephone must spend six months underground with Pluto, causing winter, and six months above ground with her mother, causing summer.

Visual Summary

Myth	"How Glooskap Found the Summer"
Culture	Algonquin
Conflict	Glooskap wants to save his people from a long Winter and gets Summer to battle Winter.
Resolution	Summer defeats Winter but agrees to allow Winter to come to Glooskap's land for part of the year.
Purpose	It explains the seasons.

Myth	"Persephone and the Pomegranate Seeds"
Culture	Ancient Greek
Conflict	Demeter, goddess of agriculture, does not want her daughter Persephone to be Pluto's bride in the underworld and gets Zeus to help.
Resolution	Zeus decides that since Persephone eats only six of the twelve pomegranate seeds, she stays in the underworld only half the year.
Purpose	It explains the seasons.

How Glooskap Found the Summer

Use What You Know

List three things you know about the seasons.

1. _____

2. _____

3. _____

Text Structure: Myth

A myth is an old story that tries to explain why something is the way it is. Most myths try to explain things in nature. Underline the words describing Winter and Summer, aspects of nature that are turned into characters in this myth. What are the lands like where Winter and Summer live?

MARK THE TEXT

_____

_____

_____

Reading Strategy: Noting Causes and Effects

A cause is a reason something happens; an effect is the result. Underline the effect of the charm Winter puts on Glooskap. What caused Glooskap to visit Winter?

MARK THE TEXT

_____

_____

What caused him to go south?

_____

_____

Long ago, the Wawaniki people lived in the northeastern part of North America. Their leader's name was Glooskap.

One time, it grew very cold. Snow and ice were everywhere, and plants could not grow. The Wawaniki began to die from the cold and **famine**. Glooskap traveled far north, where the land was all ice. He came to a **wigwam**, where he found Winter. Winter was a **giant** with icy breath. Winter's breath was so cold, it had frozen all the land. Glooskap entered Winter's wigwam and sat down. Winter told him stories of the old times, when he, Winter, ruled Earth, when all the land was white and beautiful. As Winter talked, Glooskap fell asleep. Winter **put a charm on** Glooskap, and he slept for six months.

Finally, Glooskap woke up. A wild bird named Tatler the Loon came and told him about a country in the south that was always warm. The bird said that a queen lived there who could make Winter go away. "I must save my people," Glooskap thought. So he decided to go south and find the queen.

Glooskap traveled south until he came to a warm forest with many flowers and trees. There, he found Summer, the fairy queen. Glooskap knew that Summer could make Winter go away, so he said to her, "Come with me to the land in the far north." Summer agreed to go with Glooskap.

---

famine, time when there is not enough food
wigwam, a home Native Americans often made by covering a frame with bark or animal skins
giant, very large, strong person (in myths and children's stories)
put a charm on, used his power on

When they reached Winter's wigwam, Winter welcomed them. "I'll make them fall asleep," Winter thought. But this time, Glooskap's power was stronger because Summer was with him. First, Glooskap and Summer made sweat run down Winter's face. Winter started to cry because he was losing his power. Next, Winter's icy wigwam melted. Then Summer used her power and everything woke up: The grass and flowers grew, leaves appeared on trees, and the snow ran down the rivers. "My power is gone!" Winter cried.

Then Summer said, "I have proved that I am stronger than you. So now I will give you all the country to the far north. Six months of every year you may come back to Glooskap's country. During the other six months, I will come back to his land."

"I accept your offer," Winter whispered sadly. So every autumn, Winter returns to Glooskap's country and brings cold and snow. When he comes, Summer runs home to her land in the south. But at the end of six months, Summer always returns to drive Winter away and bring back the grass, leaves, and flowers.

_____

sweat, liquid that comes out of your skin when you are hot
melted, changed from ice to water by heat
drive Winter away, make Winter go away

Choose one and complete:
1. Draw a picture or make a collage that captures a scene in either myth.
2. Draw an imaginative map showing Glooskap's or Persephone's travels. Include art showing the weather, seasons, or other conditions in the different areas they visit.

Literary Element: Hero/Heroine

A hero or heroine is a character whose actions are inspiring or noble. Underline the name of the hero of this story. In what way is his or her behavior noble or inspiring?

MARK THE TEXT

_____

_____

_____

Reading Strategy: Noting Causes and Effects

Underline three events that cause Winter to cry, "My power is gone!" How does Winter seem to feel as a result of Summer's victory?

MARK THE TEXT

_____

_____

_____

Text Structure: Myth

Underline the final conditions that Summer states and Winter agrees to. What aspect of nature does the ending attempt to explain?

MARK THE TEXT

_____

_____

_____

_____

Reading Strategy: Noting Causes and Effects

According to the first paragraph, why can't Pluto get a woman to marry him? Underline the cause. What effect does seeing Persephone have on Pluto?

MARK THE TEXT

_____

_____

_____

Comprehension Check

Circle two words in the first paragraph that describe the underworld. Why would the goddess of agriculture especially dislike the idea of her daughter living in such a place?

MARK THE TEXT

_____

_____

_____

_____

Text Structure: Myth

Underline Zeus's final decision. How does his decision supposedly explain the seasons?

MARK THE TEXT

_____

_____

_____

_____

Persephone and the Pomegranate Seeds

Long ago, Demeter, the goddess of **agriculture**, had a beautiful daughter named Persephone. Demeter helped trees and plants to grow on Earth. Pluto, the god of the **underworld**, lived under Earth, where it was always dark and cold. Pluto wanted a wife, but no one wanted to leave the sunshine to live in Pluto's dark world underground.

One day Pluto saw Persephone while she was picking flowers. He wanted to marry her, but he knew that Demeter would say no. So he rode a **chariot** and took Persephone to the underworld. As they were crossing a river, Persephone dropped her flowers into the water.

The river took the flowers to Demeter, who asked Zeus, the king of the gods, to help get Persephone back. Zeus answered, "I'll send my **messenger** Hermes to the underworld. But if Persephone eats anything there, she cannot return to Earth."

Pluto knew that if Persephone ate anything, she must stay with him. So he gave her twelve pomegranate seeds. She was very hungry and started to eat. While she was eating, Hermes arrived. "Persephone, did you eat the twelve seeds?" he inquired.

"I ate only six," she replied. Hermes didn't know what to do, so he returned to Zeus.

Zeus said, "Persephone ate six seeds, so she must stay in the underworld six months a year. She can spend the other six months on Earth with Demeter."

And that is why there are six cold months of autumn and winter each year, and six warm months of spring and summer.

---

agriculture, farming, especially growing crops
underworld, place where the spirits of the dead lived
chariot, ancient vehicle that horses pulled
messenger, someone who carries information

Retell It!

Imagine that you are retelling one of the myths out loud to an audience of young children. What changes will you make? What tone will you use? List your ideas here.

_____

_____

_____

_____

_____

_____

Reader's Response

Which of the two myths did you find more imaginative or colorful? What did you like about it?

_____

_____

_____

_____

_____

_____

Think About the Skill

How did noting causes and effects help you better understand the events and characters' behavior?

_____

_____

_____

_____

_____

_____

GRAMMAR

Use with textbook page 238.

Using Quotations

A **quotation** is a speaker's exact words repeated in a text. Quotations are set off by quotation marks (" "). To introduce a quotation, use the subject, or the name of the character, and a reporting verb. Use a comma after the reporting verb.

Subject	Reporting Verb	Quotation
Summer	whispered,	"Wake up, flowers and grass."

The subject and reporting verb can also follow the quotation. For statements, use a comma at the end of the quotation. For questions, use a question mark.

Quotation	Reporting Verb	Subject
"Mother, rescue me,"	shouted	Persephone.
"Persephone, will you marry me**?**"	asked	Pluto.

Read the sentences. Circle the name of each subject or speaker.
Draw a line under the reporting verb.

1. "I don't want to stay here!" cried Persephone.

2. The Loon shouted, "Wake up, Glooskap."

3. "Yes, I will go to the northern land with you," said
Summer.

4. "Where is my daughter?" asked Demeter.

5. "Please help us get warm," pleaded the people.

Read the sentences below. Rewrite each one, using the
correct punctuation.

6. I can't live without my daughter cried Demeter.

_____

7. Why aren't you happy inquired Pluto.

_____

8. Persephone asked When can I go home

_____

9. Our leader is brave and good, said the people.

_____

10. Do you want my help asked Summer.

_____

GRAMMAR

Use after the lesson on apostrophes with contractions and possessives.

Apostrophes with Contractions and Possessives

Apostrophes (') are used in English for two different purposes: to show that someone owns or **posseses** something and to take the place of letters in **contractions**.

Read each sentence. Find where apostrophes have been used incorrectly, cross them out, and rewrite the sentences putting the apostrophes in the right place.

Example: W~~e~~'re going to study astronomy. *We're going to study astronomy.*

1. Theyr'e different climates in different places on Earth. _____

   _____

2. The'yve created an imaginary line called the equator. _____

   _____

3. Earth's orbit is'nt really a circle. _____

   _____

4. Its' always cold around the North and South Poles. _____

   _____

5. Sunlight cant' reach the side of Earth that faces away from the sun. _____

   _____

Change each phrase into a possessive.

Example: the calendar of the Egyptians. *the Egyptians' calendar*

6. the energy of the sun _____

7. the orbits of the planets _____

8. the rotation of Earth _____

9. the wigwam of Winter _____

10. the leader of the people _____

SKILLS FOR WRITING

Use with textbook page 239.

Writing Dialogue

Conversations that take place between characters in a book or play are called **dialogue**. In a story, quotation marks are used to show dialogue. By varying your reporting verbs, you can make your writing more interesting.

Read the following sentences from the story about Persephone and Pluto. Rewrite them using dialogue. Be sure to vary your reporting verbs.

> Persephone begged Pluto to let her go back to Earth.
> She told him that she missed the sunlight.
> Pluto answered that he wanted her to be his wife to and to live with him
>   in the underworld.
> He told her that she would get used to living in darkness.
> Persephone whispered that she would die if she had to live without light.
> She needed sunshine to be happy, Persephone insisted.

Example: *"Please let me go back to Earth," Persephone begged Pluto.*

1. _____

   _____

2. _____

   _____

3. _____

   _____

4. _____

   _____

5. _____

   _____

PROOFREADING AND EDITING

Use with textbook page 240.

Read the myth carefully. Find the mistakes. Then rewrite the myth correctly on the lines below.

Why the Sea Has Tides

Long ago, two mermaids lived on opposite sides of the great sea. Both of them liked to sleep on the sand and use the sea for a blanket. But the sea was not quite big enough to stretch from one land to the other.

One day Marisol swam to see Della. I cant sleep without my watery blanket", Marisol told Della.

Della replied "I can't sleep without the blanket, either.

We should cooperate, Marisol stated. Suddenly she shouted, Ive got it!

"Tell me?" Della demanded.

Marisol explained, "we can sleep at different times and share the ocean blanket.

"So we can take turns pulling it up to cover us" said Della.

They tried out their Marisols' idea. Now every day they take turns pulling up their ocean blanket. And that is why the sea has a tide that goes back and forth.

_____

_____

_____

_____

_____

_____

_____

_____

_____

_____

SPELLING

Spelling /t/, /th/, /d/
Use after the spelling lesson.

It is easy to confuse the sound that you hear at the beginning of the word *tin* with the sound you hear at the beginning of the word *thin* and to misspell words with the letters that stand for these sounds. It is also easy to confuse the sound that you hear at the beginning of the word *Dan* with the sound you hear at the beginning of the word *than.*

Circle the word in parentheses ( ) that correctly completes each sentence.

1. The Wawaniki began to (thy/die) from the cold.

2. (Then/den) Summer used her power, and everything woke up.

3. Summer said, "I have proved that I am stronger (than/Dan) you."

4. As (they/day) were crossing the river, Persephone dropped her flowers.

5. And that is why (there/dare) are six cold
months of autumn and winter each year, and
six warm months of spring and summer.

6. Earth's (path/pat) as it revolves around the
sun is called its orbit.

7. They (thought/taut) that the sun and
moon were moving around the Earth.

8. The (fourth/fort) year has 366 days.

9. The sun's energy and (heat/heath) are less strong
at the poles.

10. It is (thought/taut) that they arranged the stones to record the
sun's movements.

UNIT 6 Observing the Universe

Contents

VOCABULARY

Use with textbook page 243.

Read each sentence. Circle the letter of the word or phrase that has the same meaning as the underlined word in the sentence.

1. The travelers were great <u>adventurers</u> who looked for excitement and new places.

   a. explorers   b. accountants   c. educators   d. teachers

2. The king's goal was to <u>conquer</u> his enemies and take their land.

   a. meet   b. beat   c. annoy   d. accept

3. We were happy when our country's team won the first Olympic tennis <u>match</u>.

   a. class   b. argument   c. flag   d. competition

4. When we were in France, we toured the incredible <u>palace</u> where King Louis XIV lived.

   a. hut   b. factory   c. castle   d. university

5. His father's <u>realm</u> was so huge, it took the prince a week to ride across it.

   a. kingdom   b. court   c. building   d. council

Read the clues. Use the words in the box to complete the crossword puzzle. (Hint: You will not use all the words.)

| places | serve | contest | adventurers |
| conquer | palace | intolerable | realm |

ACROSS
2. a king or queen's home
4. to win by force
5. a kingdom

DOWN
1. people who look for adventure
3. a competition

VOCABULARY BUILDING

Understanding Meaning Based on Word Roots

The English language has many words that come from **Greek and Latin roots**. It also has many **suffixes**, or word endings. If you know the meaning of **root words** and suffixes, they can help you figure out the meaning of the word. For example, the English word root -*scope* comes from the Greek *skopos*, which means "to look at." The English word root *aud-* comes from the Latin *audire*, which means "to hear." Look at the chart below to see how roots are combined and how roots and suffixes are combined to make new words.

Root	Meaning	+ Root or Suffix	Meaning	= New Word
tele-	far off	-scope	to look at	telescope
micro-	small	-scope	to look at	microscope
aud-	to hear	-orium	place of or for	auditorium
aud-	to hear	-ence	act or process	audience
aud-	to hear	-ion	act or process	audition

On the first line, use the meanings of the root (s) and/or suffix to write a meaning for each new word. Then find each word in a dictionary to check the meaning. Write the dictionary definition on the second line.

1. telescope _____

_____

2. microscope _____

_____

3. auditorium _____

_____

4. audience _____

_____

5. audition _____

_____

READING STRATEGY

Use with textbook page 243.

Reading Plays Aloud
By **reading a play aloud**, you bring the
characters and their story to life. The actors, who
perform the play, and the audience, who watches the
performance, enjoy the words and actions of the story.

Assign yourself a part from *The Great Bear* on pages
244–251 in your textbook. Read the play to yourself,
concentrating on your lines and stage directions.

Write the stage directions for your character and notes
about the way you plan to play the part. Think about the
ways you'll use your voice and gestures.

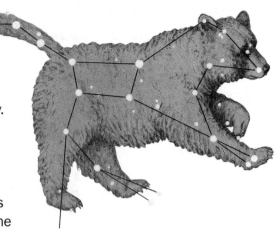

My Character	My Stage Directions	How I'll Play the Part

Now use what you wrote in the chart to answer the questions.

1. Summarize what the stage directions tell you to do.

_____

_____

2. How will you use your voice and gestures to play your role?

_____

_____

3. How has reading the whole play helped you understand your role?

_____

_____

4. Why do you think your part is important to the play as a whole?

_____

_____

_____

5. Now read Scene 1 on page 244–247 aloud. Did you understand the scene better
after you read it aloud than when you read it to yourself? Why or why not?

_____

_____

Use with textbook pages 254–256.

Summary: "Telescopes"

People use telescopes to see things that are far away, such as stars. This passage describes two kinds of telescopes and explains how they work. It also explains how readers can make simple telescopes to observe the stars.

Visual Summary

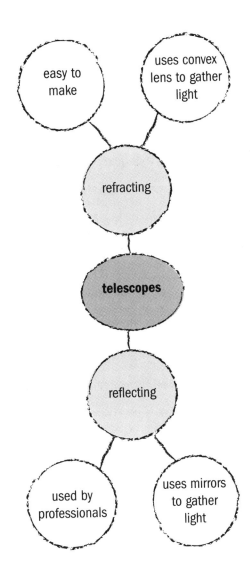

Copyright © 2004 by Pearson Education, Inc.

Use What You Know

List three things you might observe in the nighttime sky.

1. _____

2. _____

3. _____

Text Structure: Science Article

A science article gives factual information about a topic in biology, chemistry, or another science. Read the first two sentences of this article. Underline the type of scientist the article mentions. What science do you conclude the article gives information about?

_____

Reading Strategy: Skimming a Text

When you skim a text, you read it quickly to learn the main ideas. You then give it a more careful reading. Skim this page before reading it in detail. What two kinds of telescopes does it tell about?

_____

_____

Comprehension Check

Now read the page in more detail. What does each type of telescope use to collect and focus the light?

_____

_____

Telescopes

Light from the sky gives astronomers most of their information about the planets and stars. Astronomers use telescopes to collect and use this light. The more light a telescope collects, the more information it gives astronomers. There are two main kinds of telescopes that use visible light: refracting telescopes and reflecting telescopes.

Refracting Telescopes

The simplest telescope is a refracting telescope, or refractor. A refracting telescope uses a large convex lens to collect and focus a large amount of light onto a small area. A convex lens is a piece of transparent glass. It is curved so that the middle is thicker than the edges. A refracting telescope also has a smaller eyepiece lens that magnifies the images. A person uses the eyepiece lens to look through the telescope.

Reflecting Telescopes

Reflecting telescopes collect light using a curved mirror. The mirror focuses a large amount of light onto a small area. The larger the mirror, the more light the telescope can collect. Most modern professional telescopes are reflecting telescopes, with mirrors many meters wide. They are usually located in observatories on mountaintops.

---

convex lens, piece of glass curved outward (like the surface of your eye), which makes something look bigger
transparent, clear; see-through
magnifies, makes something look larger
professional, used by people with special training
observatories, buildings where astronomers watch the sky

Making a Refracting Telescope

To make a simple refracting telescope, you will need the following materials.

- 2 paper towel tubes of slightly different **diameters**
- plastic convex lens (43 mm [1.7 in.] diameter, 400 mm [16 in.] focal length)
- plastic eyepiece lens (17.5 mm [0.7 in.] diameter, 25 mm [1 in.] focal length)
- foam holder for the eyepiece, slightly larger than the diameter of the smaller tube
- transparent tape
- **meter stick** or **yardstick**

Use the following steps to make your telescope.

1. Put the smaller paper towel tube inside the other tube.

2. Place the convex lens flat against the end of the outer tube. Tape the lens in place. Try not to cover the lens with the tape.

3. Put the eyepiece lens in the middle of the foam holder. Draw a circle around the lens on the foam holder. Carefully cut the circle out of the foam holder. Put the eyepiece lens in the holder opening.

4. Trim the edge of the foam holder so that it will fit into the inner tube at the end of the telescope opposite the convex lens.

5. Tape a meter stick or yardstick to the wall. Stand 4.5 meters (5 yd.) from the wall. Look through the eyepiece. Slide the outer tube in and out to focus the telescope. Stop when you can read the numbers on the meter stick or yardstick.

---

diameters, widths of circles, measured from side to side through the center

meter stick, measuring stick 1 meter long

yardstick, measuring stick 1 yard, or 3 feet, long

Copyright © 2004 by Pearson Education, Inc.

Reading Strategy: Skimming a Text

Skim this page before reading it in more detail. What does the information on this page show readers how to do?

_____

What are the two main sections about?

_____

_____

Text Structure: Science Article

Science articles often give step-by-step instructions on how to perform scientific experiments or gather scientific information. Circle the numbered steps for making a refracting telescope. How many steps are there in the instructions?

MARK THE TEXT

_____

Comprehension Check

Circle the materials needed to make the telescope. Which of the listed materials do you think will be hardest to get? Where might you get it?

MARK THE TEXT

_____

_____

_____

_____

Using a Telescope

You can use your telescope to look at objects in the classroom and outside. **CAUTION**: *Do **not** look at the sun. You will damage your eyes.*

You can also use your telescope to observe the sky at night. Before you go outside, prepare carefully for your observations. First, decide which planets or stars you want to observe. Take along these items:

- notebook
- pen or pencil
- accurate watch
- flashlight covered with red cellophane
- telescope or binoculars
- something to sit on
- books and star maps
- small table

If the weather is cold where you live, be sure to wear warm clothing, including a warm hat and waterproof shoes. It can take up to 30 minutes for your eyes to become accustomed to the dark and to get full night vision.

Outside, the flashlight covered with red cellophane gives off a reddish light. This reddish light makes it easier to read books or star maps and to take notes. Record the time, date, and location of your observations. Make a chart in your notebook:

Planets or stars observed:	
Time:	Date:
Location:	
Observations:	

accurate, correct
cellophane, thin, clear material used for wrapping things
binoculars, pairs of glasses that you use to look at distant objects
waterproof, not allowing water to go through
become accustomed to, get comfortable with
night vision, ability to see things at night

Reading Strategy: Skimming a Text

Skim this page before reading it in more detail. What does the page tell readers how to do?

_____

_____

Comprehension Check

Underline the words in the second paragraph that tell **MARK THE TEXT** what to do first before going outside and looking at the sky. Which of the items listed after the second paragraph could help someone do this?

_____

_____

Text Structure: Science Article

Science articles often include charts and diagrams to illustrate the points they make. Circle the chart near the end of this article. What does it show? **MARK THE TEXT**

_____

_____

_____

_____

_____

_____

Name _____ Date _____

Retell It!

Give this article a more personal touch by telling about a student who reads it and then makes and uses the telescope to look at the nighttime sky. Use information from the article in your retelling.

_____

_____

_____

_____

_____

_____

_____

_____

_____

_____

Reader's Response

What did you find most interesting in this article? Why?

_____

_____

_____

_____

_____

Think About the Skill

How did skimming help you better understand the article?

_____

_____

_____

GRAMMAR

Use with textbook page 258.

Using Prepositional Phrases

A **prepositional phrase** is made up of a *preposition* + a *noun* or *pronoun*. Prepositional phrases can show location, time, or description.

Location: *under* the table   *at* school   *behind* the house   *on* the wall
Time: *at* noon   *around* midnight   *after* school   *during* vacation   *by* ten o'clock
Description: *about* the solar system   *of* the history of life   *with* a tiny lens

Underline the prepositional phrase in each sentence. Write *P* over each preposition and *N* over the noun in the prepositional phrase.

1. Gary and Nico placed their telescope on a hill.

2. They always found constellations in the evening.

3. They waited patiently under a tree.

4. Both boys had read books about constellations.

5. The sky was full of stars.

Complete each sentence with a prepositional phrase. Use the preposition in parentheses ( ).

6. I like to watch the stars _____. (at)

7. I know a lot _____. (about)

8. I bring my telescope to the top _____. (of)

9. I wait until the moon is _____. (above)

10. Lately, it comes out _____. (by)

GRAMMAR

Use after the lesson on using adverbs for precision.

Using Adverbs for Precision

Adverbs are words that describe a verb, an adjective, or another adverb. They tell us when, where, how, and how much. Adverbs are often used in science to show **precision**. Adverbs such as *slowly, carefully, neatly,* and *clearly* are used in instructions to tell us exactly what to do. Notice that many of the precision adverbs end with the letters *-ly*.

> Move the tubes *slowly* to focus the telescope.
> *Carefully* cut the circle out of the foam holder.
> Stir the mixture *well*.

Read the following instructions for making a refracting telescope. Circle the adverbs that show precision. Follow the example.

Example: Measure (exactly) the right amount of glass.

1. Put the smaller tube precisely inside the larger tube.

2. Place the convex lens flat against the end of the outer tube and neatly tape the lens in place.

3. Put the eyepiece lens in the foam holder. Draw a circle around the lens on the foam holder. Carefully cut the circle out of the foam holder. Put the eyepiece lens in the holder opening.

4. Cautiously trim the edge of the foam holder so that it will fit into the inner tube at the end of the telescope opposite the convex lens.

5. You may have to slightly adjust the mirrors in your telescope to focus it.

SKILLS FOR WRITING

Writing a Skit

Use with textbook page 259.

Read the following statements about the format of plays. Knowing about plays will help you when you write a short play, or skit. Write the letter for the correct answer in the space provided before the number.

_____ **1.** A narrator of a play _____.

    a. always provides the sound effects
    b. usually introduces, comments on, and concludes the story

_____ **2.** When you act out a play, you read the stage directions _____.

    a. out loud
    b. to yourself

_____ **3.** To find the words a character speaks in a play, look for the words _____.

    a. in parentheses
    b. not in parentheses and after a character's name

_____ **4.** To find out who the characters are in a play, you _____.

    a. usually look for a list at the beginning
    b. must always skim the play for the names

_____ **5.** The best way to find out what props (bows and arrows or other things) you'll need is to look at _____.

    a. the stage directions
    b. what the characters say to each other

_____ **6.** To find out how a character feels or what a character does, look at _____.

    a. the stage directions
    b. the punctuation marks

_____ **7.** In a play, the character's name is followed by a _____.

    a. comma (,)
    b. colon (:)

_____ **8.** What a character says in a play is _____.

    a. always in quotation marks
    b. not in quotation marks

_____ **9.** You can often find the setting of a play at the _____.

    a. beginning of a scene
    b. end of the play

_____ **10.** A scene in a play often changes when _____.

    a. a new character comes in
    b. time or place changes

PROOFREADING AND EDITING

Use with textbook page 260.

Read the skit carefully. Find the mistakes. Then rewrite the skit correctly on the lines below.

<u>First Woman Hangs the stars</u>

CHARACTERS: Narrator, First Woman, First Man, Coyote

SCENE 1

(Setting: Desert in American Southwest)

NARRATOR: Long ago, first woman and First Man gazed in the sky. It was huge and black. Brother Moon rested in the center, but there was nothing else up there.

FIRST WOMAN: The night sky is so beautiful!

FIRST MAN: *(Agrees)* Yes, Brother moon does a fine job of lighting it! *(Coyote enters)*

COYOTE: *(Slyly)* Greetings, First Woman and first Man What are you looking at

FIRST WOMAN: We're looking in the night sky! Doesn't Brother Moon do a fine job of bringing light to us at night

COYOTE: *(Shakes his head)* No, no, no, First Woman! He doesn't do a good job at all We could use some stars at the sky

NARRATOR: First Man and First Woman were puzzled. They did not know what stars were they had never seen them before.

_____

_____

_____

_____

_____

_____

_____

_____

_____

_____

Name _____ Date _____

SPELLING

Use after the spelling lesson.

Adding –ing

To add -ing to verbs, use the following rules.

- For most verbs, just add -ing to the base form of the verb.
  call, calling   shoot, shooting   try, trying
- For one-syllable verbs that have a consonant-vowel-consonant pattern, double the last consonant before adding -ing.
  get, getting   put, putting   win, winning
- For verbs that end in a silent e, drop the final e and add -ing.
  care, caring   chase, chasing   move, moving

Add -ing to each of the verbs in parentheses ( ) and write the new word in the space provided.

Example: "What are you (do) _____*doing*_____ ?" they asked Mountain Lifter.

1. Sky Shooter was (gaze) _____ up at the sky.

2. Great Listener was (listen) _____ to the earth and the sky.

3. They saw a woman (capture) _____ gazelles one by one.

4. Swift Runner was (let) _____ the gazelles go free.

5. They went out to a field where trees were (grow) _____ at one end.

6. The wrestler had trouble (pull) _____ up the trees.

7. The old woman had never been beaten at (race) _____.

8. She ran swiftly, never (stop) _____ to look back.

9. By (spit) _____ out the water, Sea Swallower saved them all.

10. They are still (live) _____ peacefully and happily in heaven.